Fallout

Methuen Drama

Published by Methuen Drama 2003

3 5 7 9 10 8 6 4

First published in 2003 by
Methuen Publishing Limited

Methuen Drama
A & C Black Publishers Limited
36 Soho Square
London W1D 3QY

www.methuendrama.com

A CIP catalogue record for this book is available from the British Library

ISBN 978 0 413 77367 8

Available in the USA from Bloomsbury Academic & Professional,
175 Fifth Avenue/3rd Floor, New York, NY 10010
www.BloomsburyAcademicUSA.com

Typeset by SX Composing DTP, Rayleigh, Essex

ROYAL COURT

Royal Court Theatre presents

FALLOUT

by **Roy Williams**

First performance at the Royal Court Jerwood Theatre Downstairs
Sloane Square, London on 12 June 2003.

Supported by Jerwood New Playwrights

JERWOOD
NEW PLAYWRIGHTS

FALLOUT

by **Roy Williams**

Cast in order of appearance

Clinton **Jason Frederick**
Dwayne **Michael Obiora**
Emile **Marcel McCalla**
Perry **O-T Fagbenle**
Joe **Lennie James**
Matt **Daniel Ryan**
Shanice **Ony Uhiara**
Ronnie **Petra Letang**
Manny **Clive Wedderburn**
Miss Douglas/Defence Lawyer **Lorraine Brunning**

Director **Ian Rickson**
Designer **Ultz**
Lighting Designer **Nigel J. Edwards**
Sound Designer **Ian Dickinson**
Music **Stephen Warbeck**
Assistant Director **Natalie Abrahami**
Casting Director **Lisa Makin**
Production Manager **Paul Handley**
Stage Manager **Nicole Keighley**
Deputy Stage Manager **Claire Lovett**
Assistant Stage Manager **Fay Mansfield**
Costume Supervisor **Iona Kenrick**
Fight Director **Terry King**
Company Voice Work **Patsy Rodenburg**
Stage configuration supplied by **Flints**

THE COMPANY

Roy Williams (writer)
For the Royal Court: Clubland, Lift Off (with RNT Studio).
Other theatre includes: Sing Yer Heart Out for the Lads (RNT); The Gift (Birmingham Repertory/ Tricycle); Local Boy (Hampstead); Souls (Theatre Centre); Starstruck (Tricycle); Josie's Boys (Red Ladder); The No-Boys Cricket Club (Theatre Royal, Stratford East); Night and Day (Theatre Venue).
Television includes: Offside, Babyfather.
Radio includes: Homeboys, Tell Tale.
Awards include: Evening Standard's Most Promising Playwright Award 2001, BAFTA Children's Film and Television Award 2002 for Offside for Best Schools Drama and nominated for BAFTA Children's Film and Television Award for Best Writer, Joint Winner of the George Devine Award 2000 for Lift Off, Winner of the 31st John Whiting Award and the 1999 EMMA Award for Starstruck.

Natalie Abrahami (assistant director)
For the Royal Court as assistant director: Caryl Churchill Season.
As director, other theatre includes: Broken Glass, Bash: Latterday Plays, Spoonface Steinberg (Cambridge University).

Lorraine Brunning
For the Royal Court: Cries From the Mammal House, Low Level Panic (& Lyric).
Other theatre includes: Lady in the Van (Queens); Piaf (Piccadilly); Rupert Street Lonely Hearts Club (Donmar/Criterion); Snoopy the Musical (Duchess); Emma (Tricycle); Long Time Gone (Lyric); Ring of Iron (Soho Poly); The Singing Group (Chelsea); The Contractor, An Inspector Calls, (Birmingham Repertory); The Rise & Fall of Little Voice (Derby Playhouse); Taste of Honey, Macbeth, Piaf (Royal Theatre, Northampton); Ten Times Table, Sisterly Feelings (Theatre Royal, Windsor); Peter Pan (Everyman, Cheltenham); Hard Times (Salisbury Playhouse); Sailor Beware (Queens, Hornchurch); Princess & the Monkey (Oxford Stage Company); Season's Greetings (Mill at Sonning).
Television includes: Home Sweet Home, Third Time Lucky, All Electric, A Killing on the Exchange, Cries, Pratt Outta Hell, The Knights, Covington Cross, Kinsey, Casualty, EastEnders, House, The Manageress, Basic, Brookside, The Rory Bremner Show, The Bill, The Miracle Men, Kissing the Gunner's Daughter, Coronation Street, Holby City.
Film includes: Personal Services, Sarah, Princess in Love, The Joke, Topsy-Turvy.

Ian Dickinson (sound designer)
For the Royal Court: Flesh Wound, Hitchcock Blonde, Black Milk, Crazyblackmuthafuckin'self, Caryl Churchill Season, Imprint, Mother Teresa is Dead, Push Up, Workers Writes, Fucking Games, Herons, Cutting Through the Carnival.
Other theatre includes: Port (Royal Exchange Manchester); Night of the Soul (RSC Barbican); Eyes of the Kappa (Gate); Crime and Punishment in Dalston (Arcola Theatre); Search and Destroy (New End, Hampstead); Phaedra, Three Sisters, The Shaughraun, Writer's Cramp (Royal Lyceum, Edinburgh); The Whore's Dream (RSC Fringe, Edinburgh); As You Like It, An Experienced Woman Gives Advice, Present Laughter, The Philadelphia Story, Wolks World, Poor Superman, Martin Yesterday, Fast Food, Coyote Ugly, Prizenight (Royal Exchange, Manchester).
Ian is Head of Sound at the Royal Court.

Nigel J. Edwards (lighting designer)
For the Royal Court: 4.48 Psychosis, Cleansed, Crave (Paines Plough and Bright Ltd tour); Bailengangaire (at the Ambassadors).
Other theatre includes: Sexual Perversity in Chicago (Comedy); One Minute (Crucible Studio, Sheffield); The Oresteia (RNT); The Tempest (European/UK tour); Victoria, Roberto Zucco, The Mysteries, Shadows (RSC); Splendour, Riddance, Sleeping Around (with Salisbury Playhouse), The Cosmonaut's Last Message (Paines Plough); The Triumph of Love (Almeida & UK tour); The Maids, Dreamtime, Counting of Years (Young Vic); Dirty Butterfly (Soho), Arabian Night (Soho & UK tour); The Misanthrope (Gate, Dublin); Romeo & Juliet (Cork/Athlone/ Dublin); Inconceivable, Mister Heracles (West Yorkshire Playhouse); The Boy Who left Home (Actors Touring Company); King Arthur (Lip Service); Peer Gynt (National Theatre of Macedonia, Skopje); Pleasure, Showtime, Speak Bitterness, Hidden J., Club of No Regrets, Emmanuelle, Enchanted, Mania and Lee (Forced Entertainment); Hold Me Down, Baldy Hopkins, Penny Dreadful; Waiting for Godot (Tottering Bipeds).
Opera includes: Jenufa (Welsh National Opera), The Maids (Lyric); Hansel & Gretel (Opera North).

O-T Fagbenle

Theatre includes: A Christmas Carol (Lyric); Ragamuffin (UK Arts International); Aladdin, My Mister Right (Theatre Royal, Stratford East); Les Blancs (Royal Exchange).
Television includes: As If, 420 Seconds of Love; EastEnders.
Film includes: Poppies.

Jason Frederick

Theatre includes: Fearless Crew, S.K.I.P, Burning Ambitions (YoungBlood Theatre Company).

Lennie James

For the Royal Court: This is a Chair, Outside of Heaven, Etta Jenks.
Other theatre includes: Raisin in the Sun (Young Vic); Two Gentlemen of Verona (Globe/New Victoria, New York); Macbeth, The Piano Lesson (Tricycle); Pericles, The Coup, Ma Rainey's Black Bottom (RNT); The Merchant of Venice (Wolsey, Ipswich); Black Ice (Derby Playhouse); No Two Ways, Something's Burning (Lyric); Waking Hours (Lyric/Library, Manchester); Short Eyes (Man in the Moon); Hamlet (Shaw); Colossus, Just Good Friends (Cockpit).
Television includes: The Leeds Story, Buried, Déjà Vu, Storm Damage, Undercover Heart, Cold Feet, Perfect Blue, People of the Forest, Out of the Blue, Thieftakers, Omnibus: Artist Unknown, A Touch of Frost, Love Hurts, Comics, Civvies, Everyman, Orchid House, Between the Cracks, Something's Burning.
Film includes: 24 Hour Party People, Lucky Break, The Martins, Snatch, Elephant Juice, Among Giants, Les Miserables, Lost in Space, Fathers, Sons and Unholy Ghosts, The Announcement.

Petra Letang

For the Royal Court: Breath Boom, Rough Road to Survival.
Other theatre includes: Beautiful Thing (Nottingham Playhouse);Generations of the Dead (Young Vic); Local Boy (Hampstead).
Television includes: Babyfather, Family Affairs.
Film includes: Wondrous Obilivion.
Radio includes: Tell Tale, Madam Bitterfly and the Stockwell Diva, Silence of the Stars.

Marcel McCalla

For the Royal Court: The One with the Oven, Parallel Lines (Imprint Young Writers Festival 2002).
Other theatre includes: Oliver Twist (Palladium).
Television includes: My Wonderful Life, Mr Charity, Grange Hill, The Bill.
Film includes: Rehab, The Big Finish.

Michael Obiora

Theatre includes: Exclude Me (Chelsea); Romeo & Juliet (Wembley Park).
Television includes: Grange Hill, The Bill, Doctors, Holby City.

Ian Rickson (director)

Ian Rickson is Artistic Director of the Royal Court.
For the Royal Court: The Night Heron, Boy Gets Girl, Mouth To Mouth (& Albery), Dublin Carol, The Weir (& Broadway), The Lights, Pale Horse, Mojo (& Steppenwolf Theater, Chicago), Ashes and Sand, Some Voices, Killers, 1992 Young Writers' Festival, Wildfire.
Other theatre includes: The Day I Stood Still (RNT); The House of Yes (The Gate); Me and My Friend (Chichester Festival Theatre); Queer Fish (BAC); First Strike (Soho Poly).
Opera includes: La Serva Padrona (Broomhill).

Daniel Ryan

Theatre includes: A Midsummer Night's Dream, Richard III, Pericles, The Changeling, Coriolanus, All's Well that Ends Well, And This Little Piggy (RSC); Life after Life (RNT); Herbal Bed (Duchess); Viva Espana (Arts); The Boys from Syracuse, Macbeth, A Midsummer Night's Dream (Regents's Park), Sugar (West Yorkshire Playhouse).
Television includes: Where the Heart Is, Hanging On, Wire in the Blood, Two Thousand Acres of Sky, Love or Money, Bob & Rose, Linda Green, Throw Away the Key, Men Only, Cops, City Central, Harbour Lights, Trial and Retribution I & II, Dangerfield, The Broker's Man, The Grove, The Bill, The Governor, Dalziel and Pascoe, Independent Man, Where the Buffalo Roam, Between the Lines, N7, Casualty, Seaforth, Peak Practice, Heartbeat, Resnick I & II, The Lawlord.
Film includes: All or Nothing, Ashes and Sand, Up on the Roof, Lipstick on Your Collar.

THE ENGLISH STAGE COMPANY
AT THE ROYAL COURT

The English Stage Company at the Royal Court opened in 1956 as a subsidised theatre producing new British plays, international plays and some classical revivals.

The first artistic director George Devine aimed to create a writers' theatre, 'a place where the dramatist is acknowledged as the fundamental creative force in the theatre and where the play is more important than the actors, the director, the designer'. The urgent need was to find a contemporary style in which the play, the acting, direction and design are all combined. He believed that 'the battle will be a long one to continue to create the right conditions for writers to work in'.

Devine aimed to discover 'hard-hitting, uncompromising writers whose plays are stimulating, provocative and exciting'. The Royal Court production of John Osborne's Look Back in Anger in May 1956 is now seen as the decisive starting point of modern British drama and the policy created a new generation of British playwrights. The first wave included John Osborne, Arnold Wesker, John Arden, Ann Jellicoe, N F Simpson and Edward Bond. Early seasons included new international plays by Bertolt Brecht, Eugène Ionesco, Samuel Beckett, Jean-Paul Sartre and Marguerite Duras.

The theatre started with the 400-seat proscenium arch Theatre Downstairs, and then in 1969 opened a second theatre, the 60-seat studio Theatre Upstairs. Some productions transfer to the West End, such as Caryl Churchill's Far Away, Conor McPherson's The Weir, Kevin Elyot's Mouth to Mouth and My Night With Reg. The Royal Court also co-produces plays which have transferred to the West End or toured internationally, such as Sebastian Barry's The Steward of Christendom and Mark Ravenhill's Shopping and Fucking (with Out of Joint), Martin McDonagh's The Beauty Queen Of Leenane (with Druid Theatre Company), Ayub Khan-Din's East is East (with Tamasha Theatre Company, and now a feature film).

Since 1994 the Royal Court's artistic policy has again been vigorously directed to finding and producing a new generation of playwrights. The writers include Joe Penhall, Rebecca Prichard, Michael Wynne, Nick Grosso, Judy Upton, Meredith Oakes, Sarah Kane, Anthony Neilson, Judith Johnson, James Stock, Jez Butterworth, Marina Carr, Phyllis Nagy, Simon Block, Martin McDonagh, Mark Ravenhill, Ayub Khan-Din, Tamantha Hammerschlag, Jess Walters, Che Walker, Conor McPherson, Simon Stephens,

photo: Andy Chopping

Richard Bean, Roy Williams, Gary Mitchell, Mick Mahoney, Rebecca Gilman, Christopher Shinn, Kia Corthron, David Gieselmann, Marius von Mayenburg, David Eldridge, Leo Butler, Zinnie Harris, Grae Cleugh, Roland Schimmelpfennig, DeObia Oparei, Vassily Sigarev and The Presnyakov Brothers. This expanded programme of new plays has been made possible through the support of A.S.K Theater Projects, the Jerwood Charitable Foundation, the American Friends of the Royal Court Theatre and many in association with the Royal National Theatre Studio.

In recent years there have been record-breaking productions at the box office, with capacity houses for Terry Johnson's Hitchcock Blonde, Caryl Churchill's A Number, Jez Butterworth's The Night Heron, Rebecca Gilman's Boy Gets Girl, Kevin Elyot's Mouth To Mouth, David Hare's My Zinc Bed and Conor McPherson's The Weir, which transferred to the West End in October 1998 and ran for nearly two years at the Duke of York's Theatre.

The newly refurbished theatre in Sloane Square opened in February 2000, with a policy still inspired by the first artistic director George Devine. The Royal Court is an international theatre for new plays and new playwrights, and the work shapes contemporary drama in Britain and overseas.

Uitz (designer)

As designer, for the Royal Court: The Night Heron, Fireface, Lift Off, Mojo (& Steppenwolf Theater, Chicago).

As designer, other theatre includes: sixteen productions for the RSC including Good (also on Broadway), The Art of Success (also Manhattan Theatre Club); The Black Prince, Me and Mamie O' Rourke, A Madhouse in Goa, Animal Crackers (West End); Slavs! (Hampstead); The Resistible Rise of Arturo Ui, Ramayana (RNT); Hobson's Choice (Young Vic); Xerxes, La Clemenza di Tito, The Rake's Progress, Die Entführung aus dem Serail (Bavarian State Opera).

As director and designer, other theatre includes: Summer Holiday (Blackpool Opera House, London Apollo, UK tour, South African tour); Jesus Christ Superstar (Aarhus and Copenhagen); Don Giovanni, Cosi fan tutte (in Japanese for Tokyo Globe); A Midsummer Night's Dream (National Arts Centre, Ottawa); Dragon (RNT); The Screens (California); The Maids, Deathwatch (co-directed RSC); The Blacks (co-directed Market Theatre Johannesburg and Stockholms Stadsteater); Perikles (Stockholms Stadsteater); Snowbull (Hampstead); The Public, The Taming of the Shrew, Pericles, Baiju Bawra, Da Boyz (Theatre Royal, Stratford East, where he is now an Associate Director).

Ony Uhiara

Television includes: MIT, Crouch, Waking the Dead, The Vice (V).

Stephen Warbeck (composer)

For the Royal Court: The Night Heron, Boy Gets Girl, Mouth To Mouth, Dublin Carol, The Glory of Living, The Lights, Harry and Me, Pale Horse, Rat in the Skull, Mojo (& Steppenwolf Theatre, Chicago), Simpatico, Some Voices, The Editing Process, The Kitchen, Blood, Greenland, Bloody Poetry, A Lie of the Mind, Built on Sand.

Other theatre includes: The Prime of Miss Jean Brodie, The Day I Stood Still, Light Shining in Buckinghamshire, An Inspector Calls, Machinal, The Mother, Roots, Magic Olympical Games, At Our Table (RNT); Alice in Wonderland, The Tempest, Romeo and Juliet, The White Devil, The Taming of the Shrew, The Cherry Orchard, Cymbeline (RSC); Proof, To The Green Fields Beyond (Donmar).

Television includes: Dreamkeepers, A Christmas Carol, Bright Hair, The Student Prince, Element of Doubt, Truth or Dare, Meat, Nervous Energy, Prime Suspect, In the Border Country, Roots, Nona, You, Me and Marley, Happy Feet, Bitter Harvest, The Changeling, Skallagrigg.

Film includes: Love's Brother, Blackball, Mystics, Secret Passage, Birthday Girl, Deséo, Charlotte Gray, Captain Corelli's Mandolin, Gabriel and Me, Billy Elliot, Quills, Very Annie Mary, Mystery Men, Fanny and Elvis, Shakespeare in Love, Heart, My Son the Fanatic, Mrs Brown, Different for Girls, Brothers in Trouble, O Mary This London, Sister My Sister.

Awards include: Academy Award and BAFTA Nomination for Best Original Musical or Comedy Score for Shakespeare in Love, 2001 AFCAP Award for Best Film Music for Quills. Stephen has also written music for many BBC Radio plays and writes for his band the hKippers and also for The Metropolitan Water Board.

Clive Wedderburn

For the Royal Court: Crazyblackmuthafuckin'self.

Other theatre includes: Volpone (Sydney Arts); Women of Troy (RNT); A Season in Hell (Tabard); Mountains (Russian tour); Tomorrow Today (Midlands Arts Centre); Boy with Beer (Man in the Moon); Othello (Corbett); Roots Rules (Birmingham Rep).

Television includes: The Bill, Buddy's Story, Look At It This Way, Black & Blue, Jackanory, Hampton Celeste, Saturday Disney.

Film includes: Knights & Emeralds.

Radio includes: Darker Face of Earth, The Faithful Heart, Much Like Yourself, Bliss & Tumble, Still Stationary.

AWARDS FOR
THE ROYAL COURT

Jez Butterworth won the 1995 George Devine Award, the Writers' Guild New Writer of the Year Award, the Evening Standard Award for Most Promising Playwright and the Olivier Award for Best Comedy for Mojo.

The Royal Court was the overall winner of the 1995 Prudential Award for the Arts for creativity, excellence, innovation and accessibility. The Royal Court Theatre Upstairs won the 1995 Peter Brook Empty Space Award for innovation and excellence in theatre.

Michael Wynne won the 1996 Meyer-Whitworth Award for The Knocky. Martin McDonagh won the 1996 George Devine Award, the 1996 Writers' Guild Best Fringe Play Award, the 1996 Critics' Circle Award and the 1996 Evening Standard Award for Most Promising Playwright for The Beauty Queen of Leenane. Marina Carr won the 19th Susan Smith Blackburn Prize (1996/7) for Portia Coughlan. Conor McPherson won the 1997 George Devine Award, the 1997 Critics' Circle Award and the 1997 Evening Standard Award for Most Promising Playwright for The Weir. Ayub Khan-Din won the 1997 Writers' Guild Awards for Best West End Play and Writers' Guild New Writer of the Year and the 1996 John Whiting Award for East is East (co-production with Tamasha).

At the 1998 Tony Awards, Martin McDonagh's The Beauty Queen of Leenane (co-production with Druid Theatre Company) won four awards including Garry Hynes for Best Director and was nominated for a further two. Eugene Ionesco's The Chairs (co-production with Theatre de Complicite) was nominated for six Tony awards. David Hare won the 1998 Time Out Live Award for Outstanding Achievement and six awards in New York including the Drama League, Drama Desk and New York Critics Circle Award for Via Dolorosa. Sarah Kane won the 1998 Arts Foundation Fellowship in Playwriting. Rebecca Prichard won the 1998 Critics' Circle Award for Most Promising Playwright for Yard Gal (co-production with Clean Break).

Conor McPherson won the 1999 Olivier Award for Best New Play for The Weir. The Royal Court won the 1999 ITI Award for Excellence in International Theatre. Sarah Kane's Cleansed was judged Best Foreign Language Play in 1999 by Theater Heute in Germany. Gary Mitchell won the 1999 Pearson Best Play Award for Trust. Rebecca Gilman was joint winner of the 1999 George Devine Award and won the 1999 Evening Standard Award for Most Promising Playwright for The Glory of Living.

In 1999, the Royal Court won the European theatre prize New Theatrical Realities, presented at Taormina Arte in Sicily, for its efforts in recent years in discovering and producing the work of young British dramatists.

Roy Williams and Gary Mitchell were joint winners of the George Devine Award 2000 for Most Promising Playwright for Lift Off and The Force of Change respectively. At the Barclays Theatre Awards 2000 presented by the TMA, Richard Wilson won the Best Director Award for David Gieselmann's Mr Kolpert and Jeremy Herbert won the Best Designer Award for Sarah Kane's 4.48 Psychosis. Gary Mitchell won the Evening Standard's Charles Wintour Award 2000 for Most Promising Playwright for The Force of Change. Stephen Jeffreys' I Just Stopped by to See The Man won an AT&T: On Stage Award 2000.

David Eldridge's Under the Blue Sky won the Time Out Live Award 2001 for Best New Play in the West End. Leo Butler won the George Devine Award 2001 for Most Promising Playwright for Redundant. Roy Williams won the Evening Standard's Charles Wintour Award 2001 for Most Promising Playwright for Clubland. Grae Cleugh won the 2001 Olivier Award for Most Promising Playwright for Fucking Games. Richard Bean was joint winner of the George Devine Award 2002 for Most Promising Playwright for Under the Whaleback. Caryl Churchill won the 2002 Evening Standard Award for Best New Play for A Number. Vassily Sigarev won the 2002 Evening Standard Charles Wintour Award for Most Promising Playwright for Plasticine. Ian MacNeil won the 2002 Evening Standard Award for Best Design for A Number and Plasticine. Peter Gill won the 2002 Critics' Circle Award for Best New Play for The York Realist (English Touring Theatre).

ROYAL COURT BOOKSHOP

The bookshop offers a wide range of playtexts and theatre books, with over 1,000 titles. Located in the downstairs Bar and Food area, the bookshop is open Monday to Saturday, afternoons and evenings.

Many Royal Court playtexts are available for just £2 including works by Harold Pinter, Caryl Churchill, Rebecca Gilman, Martin Crimp, Sarah Kane, Conor McPherson, Ayub Khan-Din, Timberlake Wertenbaker and Roy Williams.

For information on titles and special events, Email: bookshop@royalcourttheatre.com
Tel: 020 7565 5024

PROGRAMME SUPPORTERS

The Royal Court (English Stage Company Ltd) receives its principal funding from London Arts. It is also supported financially by a wide range of private companies and public bodies and earns the remainder of its income from the box office and its own trading activities.
The Royal Borough of Kensington & Chelsea gives an annual grant to the Royal Court Young Writers' Programme.

The Jerwood Charitable Foundation continues to support new plays by new playwrights through the Jerwood New Playwrights series. Since 1993 A.S.K. Theater Projects of Los Angeles has funded a Playwrights' Programme at the theatre. Bloomberg Mondays, the Royal Court's reduced price ticket scheme, is supported by Bloomberg. Over the past seven years the BBC has supported the Gerald Chapman Fund for directors.

ROYAL COURT
JERWOOD THEATRE DOWNSTAIRS

6 - 30 August 2003

The Public Theater, New York

production of

TOPDOG/ UNDERDOG

by Suzan-Lori Parks

Directed by George C. Wolfe

TOPDOG/UNDERDOG tells the story of two brothers, Lincoln and Booth. Their names, given to them as a joke, foretell a lifetime of sibling rivalry and resentment. Haunted by the past and their obsession with the street con Three Card Monte, the brothers are forced to confront the shattering reality of their future.

Supported by the Laura Pels International Foundation

JERWOOD THEATRE UPSTAIRS

19 June - 12 July 2003

FOOD CHAIN

by Mick Mahoney
Directed by Anna Mackmin

Tony's doing well for himself, and his family. But what do you do when what you own is who you are?

Supported by Jerwood New Playwrights

Box Office 020 7565 5000
www.royalcourttheatre.com

JERWOOD
NEW PLAYWRIGHTS

Since 1993 Jerwood New Playwrights have contributed to some of the Royal Court's most successful productions, including SHOPPING AND FUCKING by Mark Ravenhill (co-production with Out of Joint), EAST IS EAST by Ayub Khan-Din (co-production with Tamasha), THE BEAUTY QUEEN OF LEENANE by Martin McDonagh (co-production with Druid Theatre Company), THE WEIR by Conor McPherson, REAL CLASSY AFFAIR by Nick Grosso, THE FORCE OF CHANGE by Gary Mitchell, ON RAFTERY'S HILL by Marina Carr (co-production with Druid Theatre Company), 4.48 PSYCHOSIS by Sarah Kane, UNDER THE BLUE SKY by David Eldridge, PRESENCE by David Harrower, HERONS by Simon Stephens, CLUBLAND by Roy Williams, REDUNDANT by Leo Butler, NIGHTINGALE AND CHASE by Zinnie Harris, FUCKING GAMES by Grae Cleugh, BEDBOUND by Enda Walsh, THE PEOPLE ARE FRIENDLY by Michael Wynne, OUTLYING ISLANDS by David Greig and IRON by Rona Munro. This season Jerwood New Playwrights are supporting UNDER THE WHALEBACK by Richard Bean, FLESH WOUND by Ché Walker, FALLOUT by Roy Williams and FOOD CHAIN by Mick Mahoney.

The Jerwood Charitable Foundation is a registered charity dedicated to imaginative and responsible funding and sponsorship of the arts, education, design and other areas of human endeavour and excellence.

HERONS by Simon Stephens
(photo: Pete Jones)

EAST IS EAST by Ayub Khan-Din
(photo: Robert Day)

For Donna Daley

Characters

Shanice, late teens, black
Emile, late teens, black
Dwayne, late teens, black
Joe, mid-thirties, black
Matt, mid-thirties, white
Perry, late teens, mixed race
Ronnie, late teens, black
Clinton, late teens, black
Miss Douglas, early forties, white
Inspector, early forties, white
Manny, late thirties, black

The roles of Miss Douglas and the Inspector should be played by the same actor.

Time
Present

Setting
Various

Enter **Clinton**, **Dwayne**, **Emile** *and* **Perry**.

Clinton   Kick him in the head, kick him!

Dwayne   Yes!

Perry   My bwoi.

Clinton   Kick him.

Dwayne   Tek off him glasses and chuck dem.

Clinton   Chuck dem now, man.

Emile   Pass me de phone, yu fucker!

Clinton   Pass him de phone, yu fuck!

Emile   Pass it now.

Perry   Do it now.

Dwayne   My bwoi!

Emile   Trainers too.

Clinton   Gwan, Emile!

Perry   Walk barefoot, yu rass.

Clinton   Like yu do in Africa.

Emile   Trainers!

Clinton   Tell him, Emile.

Perry   Tell the fucker.

Dwayne   Bus his head.

Clinton   Bus him up.

Emile   Trainers!

Dwayne   Fuck dem over to us.

Clinton   Before yu dead.

Emile   Trainers!

Dwayne   Punch him.

Clinton   Kick him.

Perry   Bus him up.

Emile   Yu see yu! (*Kicks continuously.*)

Exit **Clinton**, **Dwayne**, **Perry** *and* **Emile**.

Enter **Shanice** *and* **Ronnie**, **Joe** *and* **Matt**.

Ronnie   Yer gonna love me, Shanice.

Shanice   I love yer awready, yu fool.

Ronnie   Well, yer gonna love me more, dread. See?
(*Shows a blouse.*)

Shanice   Nice.

Ronnie   Honestly?

Shanice   Honestly.

Ronnie   Yes.

Shanice   Bit small fer yu.

Ronnie   Got it fer yu.

Shanice   Ronnie!

Ronnie   It'll go nice wid yer black skirt, yer gonna look
the business, girl, no guy can refuse yu.

Shanice   Don't let Emile hear yu.

Ronnie   Try it on.

Shanice   Ronnie, wat am I doin right now?

Ronnie   Nuttin.

Shanice   I'm workin.

Ronnie   Shut up.

Shanice   Later.

Ronnie   Yeah, but I want see how well it fit.

Shanice   Why yu aways gettin me things, man?

Ronnie   It don't look right on me.

Shanice   So why buy it?

Ronnie   I didn't buy it.

Shanice   Ronnie, yu didn't?

Ronnie   I saw it in the shop.

Shanice   Oh man.

Ronnie   As soon as I lay my eye upon it, I thought of yu.

Shanice   Is it?

Ronnie   It was callin to me, Shanice.

Shanice   Shush.

Ronnie   I had to have it . . .

Shanice   Hold it down.

Ronnie   Why?

Shanice (*aside*)   Police.

Ronnie   Ware?

Shanice   Deh.

Ronnie   Wat, dem?

Shanice   Yes.

Ronnie   Yo!

Shanice   Ronnie!

Ronnie   Yo!

Matt   Yes?

Ronnie   Yu lot still here?

Matt   Can we help you?

Ronnie   Yu best go home. Aint no criminals in here.

Matt   Is it written all over our foreheads or something?

Joe   How did you know?

Shanice   It's written all over yer foreheads.

Ronnie   Believe.

Shanice   Kwame?

Matt   That's right.

Ronnie   Don't yu lot get tired? Bin interviewin everyone, man. Over and over. How come yu Feds never come see me? Especially dat cute young one, wathimname. Oh man, yu should see him, Shanice. Not like these two. Bring him round, let him talk to me.

Joe   Who?

Matt   PC Adams, he has been getting this all month.

Ronnie   So yu like it den?

Shanice   It's awright.

Ronnie   Ca if yu don't like it . . .

Shanice   Wat, yu'll tek it back?

Ronnie   I'll get yu summin else.

Shanice   Yu stay ware yu are. Yeah, wat yu havin?

Joe   Two teas and a smile.

Shanice *feigns a smile.*

Joe   How big are dem chicken wings?

Shanice   I dunno, they're chicken wings.

Joe   Lemme have four.

Shanice   Comin wid yer tea.

Ronnie   No, try it on first.

Shanice   Shut up.

Ronnie   Come on.

Shanice   Awright! Love to go on. Keep an eye out.

Exit **Shanice**.

Ronnie   So, when are yu gonna send dat nice copper round to see me den?

Joe   What are you gonna tell him?

Ronnie   Watever he wants. Yu get me? (*Laughs*.)

Her phone rings.

(*Answers*.) Tracey! Wass up, girl? Hold up. (*To* **Joe** *and* **Matt**.) Keep an eye out.

Exit **Ronnie**.

Matt   Who let that out?

Joe   I like the other one.

Matt   Bit young for you.

Joe   Look me in the eye and tell me you wouldn't tap that.

Matt   I have a sister her age.

Joe   You've got a dick your age.

Matt   And a wife. What?

Joe   Something I heard.

Matt   Well, don't keep me hanging, Joe, let's have it.

Joe   A story I heard.

Matt   Yes?

Joe   When you were at Kilburn. PC Holmes was her name. Tits this big.

Matt   Nothing happened.

Joe   Oh yes?

Matt   We were friends.

Joe   No such thing.

Matt   I wasn't even married then.

Joe   You were engaged.

Matt   Are you always like this?

Joe   You must have heard what they said about me.

Matt   And they were right.

Joe   You don't have to like me, Matt.

Matt   Well, I do. Did you read the file?

Joe   I flipped through it. All this must be kicking your arse by now.

Matt   That's one way.

Joe   Funeral's tomorrow.

Matt   I know.

Joe   You going?

Matt   The super is.

Joe   Royalty.

Matt   You saw the Jubilee celebrations. We're all trying to be modern now. Shall we start?

Joe   You're the boss.

Matt   Kwame left the station at five forty-five. CCTV clocked him walking past the church towards the high street. Another one picked him up coming off the high, walking towards the swimming baths. He was inside for an hour. He went there, every Thursday. CCTV again, clocked him leaving the baths at 6.50 p.m. He bought a burger and chips from here at seven, left this place at seven ten. He was last seen walking towards the station, passing the church again. We assume he was going home. Seven fifteen. He was found at the bottom of the road.

Joe   Seven twenty-five.

Matt   It was like his head was used for a football. He died, two days later. There was another CCTV, but it wasn't working properly that evening, typical. It kept getting jammed. All it got was a lamp-post shining in its lens. We're bringing in a specialist, see if he can do anything, just like what we did for that missing girl. One witness says he saw a young man matching Kwame's description arguing with a group of boys earlier that evening. He also saw a silver BMW several times driving around the area playing really loud rap music. It was like the driver was lost or something. Whoever that driver was, he or she may have seen something, but so far, no one has come forward. Feel up to speed?

Enter **Ronnie**.

Joe   I wonder what the fight was about.

Matt   There was no fight.

Joe   Drugs. Phones.

Matt   That doesn't compute.

Joe   Why?

Matt   He was a straight-A student. On his way to university. He wasn't into gangs at all. We asked everyone, they all said the same thing, his nose was in the books.

Joe   He must have been fighting about something with them.

Matt   It wasn't a fight our witness saw, it was an argument.

Joe   So what was the argument about?

Matt   I don't know.

Enter **Clinton, Emile, Dwayne** *and* **Perry**.

Emile   Troll? Ware's Shanice?

Ronnie   Kiss my arse.

Dwayne   Shut up, troll, and tell him.

Ronnie   How am I supposed to do dat with my mouth shut? And I aint no troll.

Dwayne   Sorry, Shrek.

Laughter.

Perry   My stomach is empty.

Emile   Troll. Food.

Ronnie   Yu'll have to wait.

Perry   Tower burger, large fries.

Clinton   Is dat wat yer gonna have?

Perry   Yes, Clinton, dass wat I'm gonna have, dass why I ordered it.

Clinton   Yu had a kebab an hour ago.

Perry   I'm still hungry.

Clinton   Don't see how.

Emile   Oh man, not again.

Dwayne   Shut up, Clinton.

Clinton   Tower cheeseburger is a lot to eat by yerself.

Perry   Clinton? Yu want me to order fer yu?

Clinton   I didn't say dat.

Perry   Dis bwoi drive me mad, yu know.

Clinton   But did I say dat?

Perry   Do yu want me to order fer yu? Why yu love to go round the block wid dis?

Clinton   Wid wat?

Perry Now he's tekin the piss. Yer broke, yeah? Yu aint got enuff dollars to buy a meal. Why yu can't ask?

Clinton Don't get vex, P.

Perry I don't know why yu can't say wat yu wanna say?

Clinton Which is wat?

Perry Does dis bwoi wanna die?

Clinton If yu can't eat all dat by yerself, P, I'll help yu out.

Dwayne (*laughs*) Bredren!

Emile Oh juss help the college bwoi out P. Can't you see, he's wastin away?.

Perry It's aways me he does dis to.

Emile He's yer cousin.

Perry Dat aint my fault.

Clinton *stares*.

Perry Wat?

Clinton Nuttin.

Perry Yu want sum?

Clinton Yu don't have to.

Perry I go ask yu again. Yu gimme more than yes or no, I go bus yer head. Yu want sum food?

Clinton Yeah.

Perry Gw'y.

Laughter.

Dwayne Cold!

Clinton I knew yu'd do dat.

Perry Troll, give the bwoi sum food.

Clinton   Nice one cous.

Perry   Get a job, man.

Dwayne   Gimme a number-one meal.

Emile   Number two.

Perry   Wat yu want?

Clinton   Only if yer sure.

Perry   Pick a number before I kill yu.

Clinton   Two.

Perry   And a one fer me.

Ronnie   Yu lot mus be deaf.

Emile   Yu wan' die?

Matt (*gets up*)   Hey.

Emile   Yu want tek yer hand off my jacket please?

Matt   Take it easy, son.

Emile   Who dis fool?

Ronnie   5–0.

Emile   Oh! So dass wat de smell was.

Enter **Shanice**.

Shanice   Yeah, I like dis one. Fits nice. Awright, Emile?

Emile   Ware yu bin?

Shanice   Out back.

Dwayne   Like yer top, Shanice.

Shanice   Go away, Dwayne.

Dwayne   But it look good.

Emile   I didn't get yu dat.

Shanice   Yu don't have to get me everythin, Emile, I bought it myself.

Ronnie   No yu didn't, I got it.

Emile   Tell it to shut up.

Ronnie   Shut up yerself.

Shanice   Ronnie! Yu like it?

Dwayne   Love it.

Clinton   Believe.

Shanice   Emile?

Emile   It's awright.

Dwayne   Dass it, awright? Yer gal look fine.

Shanice   He don't like it.

Ronnie   Shanice, don't, man, it look good.

Shanice   I'm changin.

Exit **Shanice**.

Dwayne (*mocks*)   It's awright!

Perry   Emile man, yer lucky yer my bredren. Ca if yu weren't, I woulda dived on yer gal from time.

Clinton   Not before me.

Perry   Yu go down on it, Emile?

Dwayne   Cold.

Perry   She give good shine?

Emile   Shut up.

Perry   Ease up, blood.

Emile   I'm tellin yer.

Clinton   Soff.

Perry   Go sit over deh, if yu go cry.

Ronnie   See, aint juss me who tinks yer a pussy.

Emile   Yu don't shut yer mout, troll.

Ronnie   Wat?

Enter **Shanice**.

Shanice   Oh man, will yu two stop. Every time.

Dwayne   Put the other top back on.

Shanice   So yu can stare down it all night?

Perry   Believe.

Emile   Rah, he's still starin.

Clinton   Who?

Emile   Mr White Man over deh. Yu like my friend, Mr White Man? Yu want ask him out, get his number?

Joe *sucks his teeth.*

Emile   Sorry, brudda, we didn't quite catch dat. Wat, yu can't speak till him tell yu to?

Joe   Bwoi.

Emile   Yer the bwoi.

Dwayne   So wat yu doin here, Mr Policeman?

Matt   Having a tea.

Clinton   They're here fer Kwame, ennit?

Dwayne   Nuh, Clinton, really?

Emile   Wastin yer time, man, yu aint gonna catch dem.

Joe   Them?

Emile   Wat?

Joe   You said them.

Emile   I know wat I said.

Joe   Them, as in more than one?

Clinton   Guy cussin yu, Emile.

Perry   He thinks yer stupid.

Emile   Yu tink I'm stupid?

Joe   What makes you think we're looking for more than one person?

Emile   I don't.

Joe   So why say it?

Emile   I say wat I like.

Joe   True, but why say that?

Emile   Ca I felt like it.

Dwayne   Easy, dread.

Joe   Choose your words carefully.

Emile   Yu my dad now?

Joe   Maybe, wass yer mudda's name?

Clinton   Oh shame.

Matt   Joe?

Emile   Wass he say?

Clinton   He's cussin yer mum.

Shanice   Sit down, Emile.

Joe   Yes, Emile, sit down.

Emile   Go chat wid yer gal deh.

Perry   I hate to break dis to yer, Dwayne. Yer dad's comin, dis way.

Dwayne   Oh man, wass he want? He bin stalkin me all day. Don't let him in.

Manny, Dwayne's *dad, enters.*

Manny   Hey, son! Son? Ware yu going? Come here, son?

Dwayne   Wat yu want?

Manny   Lemme have one pound. Beg yu fer one pound.

Dwayne   Come outta my face, yeah.

Manny   Hey, bwoi.

Dwayne   Come outta my face!

Manny   Yer too rude, yer nuh.

Exit **Manny**.

Dwayne   Jesus man, he's an itch I can't scratch, a pain in the arse.

Perry, *by the door, laughs.*

Dwayne   Wat yu laughin at now, yu baboon?

Perry   Jamal mek me laugh, man.

Dwayne   Jamal still in Feltham.

Perry   No, he come out lass month.

Dwayne   So wat yu laughin about?

Perry   Ca he's over deh, breakin into sumone's car. Have a look. The man love to steal cars, he muss have a hard-on fer it.

Dwayne   But he always get catch.

Perry   Exactly! The guy can't even drive properly. I was in a car wid him one time, half the time we were on the pavement. But deh's no tellin him. Guy tinks he's Formula One.

Clinton   Yo, policeman, I hope dat aint yer car outside.

Matt   What car?

Clinton   Light blue Escort.

Matt Oh what! (*Jumps up.*)

Dwayne Oh yes, run, run!

Perry Why yu tell him?

Clinton I want see dis.

Dwayne Come.

Exit **Matt** *and* **Joe**.

Dwayne Yes, bwoi, run.

Perry Bredren stole a police car! Deh gonna throw his arse in prison again and keep it deh. Fer trut.

Dwayne He run fast.

Clinton Too late, yu fool.

Dwayne Come, let's go, I want see dis. Emile?

Emile I catch up.

Dwayne Yeah, go sex yer woman.

Exit **Dwayne, Clinton** *and* **Perry**.

Emile (*to* **Ronnie**) Out.

Ronnie *sucks her teeth.*

Shanice Ronnie.

Exit **Ronnie**.

Shanice *and* **Emile** *kiss.*

Shanice Missed yu.

Emile Missed yu too. I love yer hands. Did I ever tell yu dat? Yu got lovely hands.

Shanice *laughs*

Emile Wat? Yu think dat was funny?

Shanice No.

Emile   So why laugh?

Shanice   Ca yu mek me smile.

Emile   Shut up, man

Shanice   Yu do.

Emile   Yer tekin the piss.

Shanice   If yu don't like it, don't say it.

Emile   I won't.

Shanice   But I want yu to.

Emile   Look, don't wear dat top again.

Shanice   Oh man.

Emile   Juss don't.

Shanice   I knew yu didn't like it.

Emile   So why wear it?

Shanice   Ronnie got me it, yu know wat she's like.

Emile   Why yu still wid her?

Shanice   She's harmless, man. She aint got nobody.

Emile   So?

Shanice   Can we not fight please?

Emile   Sorry, yeah.

Shanice   Yu will be.

Emile   Shut up, man.

Shanice *and* **Emile** *kiss again.*

Shanice   Yu ordered yet?

Emile   Yeah, number two.

Shanice   Number two?

Emile   I'm hungry.

Shanice   Yu fat bloater.

Emile   Shut up, I aint fat.

Shanice   Hate to break it to yer, Emile, but yer gettin a little bit wide in the gut department. Anyhow, yu turn into one a dem big fat men who can hardly walk, I'll step.

Emile   Yu won't leave me.

Shanice   Yu wan bet?

Emile   Yu love me.

Shanice   I know I love yer, juss as long as yu don't turn fat on me. Oderwise, I juss have to go and check one a yer brers dem.

Emile   Yu aint jokin.

Shanice   Course I'm jokin.

Emile   Yu really tink I'm gettin fat?

Shanice   Yu are so easy to tease.

Emile   Do yer?

Shanice   No.

Emile   Yu shouldn't say dat.

Shanice   It was a joke, I'm sorry.

Emile   Wat if one a dem had heard yer?

Shanice   I don't care.

Emile   They'd dive on yu like dat, if they had the chance.

Shanice   Let dem try.

Emile   Dwayne man, he wants yer.

Shanice   Well I don't want him, I got wat I want.

Emile (*slaps her hand away*)   Move!

Shanice   Emile! Yer wrong anyway. I aint Dwayne's type.

Emile   Oh shut up, yeah.

Shanice   Yu shut up.

Emile   Yer everybody's type. Yer so fit.

Shanice   Awright.

Emile   Yer are.

Shanice   Yes! I'm fit. (*Beat.*) Wass botherin yu?

Emile   Saw Kwame's mum yesterday. Stuck up, man, always was. Lookin down on me like I'm shit. Come like her bwoi, well, he find out, ennit.

Shanice   Don't.

Emile   See her face in the paper, appealin fer help. Den deh got de blasted funeral tomorrow, why can't she juss let it go, man? She don't even live round here no more.

Shanice   Her son's dead, she can't let it go.

Emile   I thought yu were on my side.

Shanice   I am.

Emile   Well, show it den.

Shanice   Wat do yu think I'm doin?

Emile   I keep seein him.

Shanice   Shush.

Emile   His face, man.

Shanice   He'll go soon. He'll go.

Beat.

Emile   Put the oder top back on.

Shanice   Yu hate it.

Emile (*smirks*)   It look good.

Exit **Shanice** *and* **Emile**.

Enter **Matt** *and* **Joe**.

Joe   So what did they say?

Matt   They dumped the car about a mile away. They shat all over the back seats. I mean, there's no need for that.

Joe   They don't make teenagers like they used to. They ought to burn that fucker down.

Matt   I'm sorry?

Joe   The estate.

Matt   It's not the estate, it's the people.

Joe   Them as well. Young ones anyway.

Matt   Are you trying to provoke me, Joe?

Joe   Provoke?

Matt   How am I supposed to react to that?

Joe   We're all friends here, you act how you feel.

Matt   And then what?

Joe   You're losing me.

Matt   Am I supposed to agree with you?

Joe   Do you?

Matt   No.

Joe   That's exactly why they took your car. They can see right through you. Take it easy! Do you think it was them who attacked Kwame?

Matt   Well, they fit the description.

Joe   I'm surprised you can tell. You can't tell them apart in the day now, let alone night-time.

Matt   Excuse me?

Joe   Joke.

Matt   I don't find that funny.

Joe   Sorry.

Matt   Our witness named one of them.

Joe   Which one?

Matt   The leader. Dwayne Edwards.

Joe   I thought it might have been the one who goes out wid the girl. What's a nice-looking gal doing with a little bwoi like that?

Matt   I couldn't say.

Joe   I'm going to get a headache tonight, just thinking about it.

Matt   Shall we go?

Joe (*smiles*)   You're very polite.

Matt   Thank you.

Exit **Joe** *and* **Matt**.

Enter **Ronnie** *and* **Shanice**.

Shanice   Twenty grand!

Ronnie   Tellin yu.

Shanice   Fer Kwame?

Ronnie   Yes! Yu know wat I'll do if I had dat money?

Shanice   Tell me.

Ronnie   Buy car.

Shanice   Yu can't even drive.

Ronnie   I'd buy it fer yu. Get sum clothes. Yu can tell me wat to buy, dress me up.

Shanice   I don't think the world is ready fer yu in a dress.

Ronnie We go ravin every night. Hunt fer sum bwois. But only if deh buff.

Shanice Of course. So wat about Dwayne?

Ronnie Mek him jealous, ennit? Emile as well. Can't wait, man. If yu weren't goin out wid him, we could claim dat money right now.

Shanice Yu shouldn't say things like dat.

Ronnie True though.

Shanice I don't care if it's true, don't say it.

Ronnie Yeah, but it's true.

Shanice Shut up.

Ronnie Yu sound like Emile.

Shanice Sorry.

Ronnie Call me troll while yer at it.

Shanice Are yu deaf, wat did I juss say? I've never called yu dat, not even behind yer back. Ronnie, have yu told anyone wat yu saw?

Ronnie No.

Shanice Promise me.

Ronnie I haven't.

Shanice It's important.

Ronnie I know.

Shanice Ca we aint at school no more, I can't aways be deh fer yu.

Ronnie I know.

Shanice Gotta think fer yerself.

Ronnie I said I know.

Shanice Be careful wid wat yu say.

Ronnie Wat yu gettin wound up fer? Yu didn't do it.

Shanice I feel as though I have.

Ronnie Behave, man.

Shanice I had him cryin his eyes out to me.

Ronnie Wat again?

Shanice Goin on about seein Kwame's face.

Ronnie Wuss.

Shanice He aint the only one, dread. I'm seein Kwame too, every day. Him standin right here. Him leavin, wavin to me. I'm the lass person who saw him alive, Ronnie.

Ronnie No yu aint.

Shanice Yu know wat I mean. He had his lass food in here, double cheeseburger, large fries and a Coke. Dat was the lass food he ever had, double cheeseburger.

Ronnie I don't know why yu gettin stressed.

Shanice It's runnin thru my head, every day. Shit won't go.

Ronnie I know it won't, ca yu love to chat about it.

Shanice Why did Emile have to do it?

Ronnie Ask him.

Shanice Juss ignore me, yeah.

Ronnie I know wat yu need.

Shanice Tell me.

Ronnie Barbados.

Shanice (*laughs*) Is it?

Ronnie Definitely. Go stay wid yer gran. I'll come wid yu, yeah.

Shanice We go chase, man?

Ronnie   Trust.

Shanice   Awright.

Ronnie   We go swimmin.

Shanice   Bacardi Breezer.

Ronnie   Tropical Lime.

Shanice   Ruby Grapefruit.

Ronnie   Lie on beach.

Shanice   Sun in my face.

Ronnie   Yu see?

Shanice   Oh Ronnie, man! If only.

Ronnie   We can, yu know.

Shanice   No, we can't. Come on, enuff daydreamin.
Clean up.

Ronnie   Yer gonna love me, Shanice.

Shanice   I love yu awready.

Ronnie   Well, yer gonna love me even more.

Shanice   Wat yu teif now?

Ronnie   Nuttin. Guess who I saw? Guess?

Shanice   I don't want to guess, juss tell me.

Ronnie   Miss Douglas.

Shanice   Is it?

Ronnie   The slag herself.

Shanice   She see yu?

Ronnie   Yeah, she saw me.

Shanice   So wat she have to say fer herself?

Ronnie   Nuttin. She was comin outta Tesco's when I clocked her. She couldn't get across dat road fast enuff. She was clutchin her bag, like they do, well desperate to get away from me. She nearly walk right into the side of dis car, nearly get run over. Man scream out from his window, cussin her, I goes, yes, blood, tell her. I kept followin her though.

Shanice   She didn't see yu?

Ronnie   No, I was careful. Yu wanna know ware she lives now? Ashwood Gardens.

Shanice   Aint much help without a number.

Ronnie   Twenty-nine C. Yu gonna get her, Shanice? I'm comin wid yu, yeah, I have to come wid yu.

Shanice   Calm yerself.

Ronnie   I'm juss sayin, I'm comin wid yu. Let's get her back, man, let's do her good, fer kickin us out. Please Shanice?

Shanice   Awright!

Ronnie   Yes!

Joe *enters.*

Ronnie   Wass my man doin here?

Shanice   Yu here again?

Joe   No, it's what can I get you? You won't get many customers talking like that.

Ronnie   Chat is dry.

Joe   Let me have a coffee please.

Ronnie   Buff dough.

Shanice   I don't think so.

Ronnie   Oi oi buff bwoi!

Shanice   Yu mad?

Ronnie   Yu tellin me yu wouldn't?

Shanice   He's 5–0.

Ronnie   So yu would, if he wasn't? How old are yu?

Shanice   Ronnie!

Ronnie   How old?

Joe   Old enough.

Ronnie   Thirty-five or summin. Has to be. Yu look good though, fer an old man.

Shanice   Thirty-five aint dat old.

Ronnie   She thinks yer buff.

Shanice   Will yu stop shamin me.

Ronnie   So ware's the oder one?

Joe   My partner?

Ronnie   No! My man's butters. The oder one. Fit one who wears uniform. Looks like Duncan from Blue. Yu should see dis guy, Shanice.

Shanice   Yu told me.

Ronnie   Oh man!

Shanice   Yu mind? Don't go creamin yer knickers in here.

Ronnie   So ware is he?

Joe   You mean PC Adams?

Ronnie   Yeah, him, ware is he?

Joe   I have no idea. I don't know him.

Ronnie   Well, yu can find out fer me.

Shanice   Yu love to drool. Yu don't feel slack?

Ronnie   Yu should see him dough.

Shanice   Since when yu go fer white bwois? Yu muss be well moist.

Ronnie   Juss tell him I gonna come lookin fer him. It's gonna be me and him soon, tellin yu. 'Me so horny . . .

Shanice   '. . . me so sexy . . .

Ronnie/Shanice   '. . . me love yu long time!'

Laughter from the girls.

Ronnie   Wanna share him, Shanice?

Shanice   I don't do white men.

Ronnie   But if yu had to, who would yu go fer?

Shanice   None.

Ronnie   Shut up.

Shanice   None, right.

Ronnie   If I put a gun to yer face, yu still wouldn't choose?

Shanice   No.

Ronnie   Lie bad.

Shanice   White bwois too soff.

Ronnie   Blah, blah, bloody blah, who would yu choose?

Shanice   David Rees.

Ronnie   David Rees!

Shanice   Yu have to shout?

Ronnie   Oh shame.

Shanice   Only if I had to.

Ronnie   Oh yes?

Shanice   Yu open yer mout to anyone, and yu die.

Ronnie   I can see dat, yu and him.

Shanice   Aint gonna happen.

Ronnie   Oh but he's nice, really sweet and dat.

Shanice   Oh don't chat like a white girl, please.

Ronnie   I reckon he looks like Will Young.

Shanice   No!

Ronnie   Only ca him gay.

Shanice   He don't look like Will Young!

Ronnie   Ask him out.

Shanice   Move.

Ronnie   I know his brudda.

Shanice   Don't involve me in yer stupidness.

Ronnie   Yu might be missin out.

Shanice   On wat?

Ronnie   He might have a P.H.D., yu get me?

Shanice   A white bwoi?

Ronnie   Why not? Aint juss bruddas who have dem. I know sum bruddas who don't have dem. Yu have one?

Joe   What?

Ronnie   P.H.D.?

Shanice (*laughing*)   Shut up, Ronnie man.

Ronnie   Bet he don't.

Shanice   Yu don't feel no shame.

Ronnie   Watch my man's face turn red now.

Shanice   Oi, go and get sum change fer me.

Ronnie   Oh I see.

Shanice   No yu don't see.

Ronnie   Want sumtime alone wid yer man here. I'm tellin Emile. How yu know he aint here to chirps me?

Shanice   He aint chirpsin neither of us.

Ronnie   All the shops are shut.

Shanice   Costcutter's aint.

Ronnie   Dass miles.

Shanice   Pound coins and twenties.

Ronnie   Awright, I'm gone. Comin back dough. She go eat yu alive, dread.

Exit **Ronnie**.

Shanice   She's mad.

Joe   No need to apologise.

Shanice   I aint, I'm juss sayin she's mad. So ware is he?

Joe   Who, Adams? I don't know him.

Shanice   Yer partner.

Joe   Conducting interviews or something. I don't know. I gave him the slip.

Shanice   Naughty.

Joe   When you hear him ask the same questions 'bout twenty times, it gets a bit boring, you know.

Shanice   Is it?

Joe   You're a bit young to be running this place on your own.

Shanice   Is it?

Joe   Should be at school.

Shanice   Is it?

Joe   Oh, I see, you don't want chat to no policeman.

Shanice   Is . . .

Joe   . . . Is it? Beat you.

Shanice   Gimme summin worth chattin about.

Joe   Did you go to his funeral today?

Shanice   His parents wouldn't want me deh.

Joe   Why's that?

Shanice   They don't want none of the kids from round here deh.

Joe   Can't say I blame them. I wouldn't want a whole heap of kids comin to my boy's funeral when I know it's one of them that killed him, or know who did.

Shanice   I don't know who kill him.

Joe   I never said you did. Did yu know him?

Shanice   Course I knew him.

Joe   How well did you know him?

Shanice   I answered dis awready.

Joe   Yeah, but do it fer me. I'm new. Please.

Shanice   We were at school togeder.

Joe   He was attacked after leaving here.

Shanice   Yes!

Joe   How did he seem?

Shanice   Awright, he was fine.

Joe   He was here for ten minutes.

Shanice   He had to wait fer his food.

Joe   Wat did you talk about?

Shanice   Stuff, his college and that.

Joe   College?

Shanice   He had to leave home, he was scared about going away.

Joe   That's quite a conversation to have in ten minutes.

Shanice   Is it?

Joe   Was he a regular, Shanice?

Shanice   He aways used to pop in here after he went swimmin. He would sit down deh, read one of his books. Kept tellin him.

Joe   Telling him what?

Shanice   About his books. Guy loved to study, man.

Joe   And what is so wrong wid that?

Shanice   He was aways gettin teased.

Joe   By who?

Shanice   Bwois.

Joe   What boys? The same ones who were in here the other day?

Shanice   And others. Dass the way it was at school. Yu strut round wid books in yer hands, yer askin to get beat up.

Joe   Or killed.

Shanice   Aint wat I said.

Joe   I know.

Shanice   He loved to carry on, like he was better.

Joe   What's wrong wid that?

Shanice   Sum people don't like dat.

Joe   What people?

Shanice   I'm juss sayin.

Joe   Like yer boyfriend?

Shanice   He couldn't tek a joke.

Joe   How so?

Shanice   One time we had dis new teacher in, yeah. So we all decided to play a joke on him. No one was gonna speak fer the whole lesson, not do any work, juss stare out, see wat happens, wat he does. Everyone was up fer it right, except Kwame. Deh he was, sittin deh, doin his work. He ruined the joke.

Joe   He wanted to work.

Shanice   It was juss a joke.

Joe   It was his choice, he didn't have to, if he didn't want to.

Shanice   Den he was a fool. I could tell yu oder tings 'bout him.

Joe   So tell me.

Shanice   Yu don't wanna know, yu juss want catch the guy who did it.

Joe   So, I'm lookin for a guy?

Shanice   No. I don't know.

Joe   Tell me.

Shanice   First day he come to our school, teacher put him next to me, so I had to look after him. I ask him, why me?

Joe   Because you have a nice face?

Shanice   Yeah.

Joe   You have.

Shanice   Yu come like my gran.

Joe   How so?

Shanice   Ca she aways sayin, sum people have it in their nature to be nice. No matter wat they do to hide it, it's aways deh. They can't help it. Well, I could help it, I didn't want no smelly-head African next to me, followin me. I told him to move, nuff times, but he wouldn't go. I felt sorry fer him after a while, especially when other kids would start on him.

Joe   You looked after him.

Shanice   A little bit of kindness I give him, yeah, and wass he go and do, go round tellin everyone I'm his girlfriend, he tries to plant a kiss on me, comin out wid shit dat West Indian women are fast and loose, not as pure as African women like his mum, I tell him to tek his bony-arsed, black-as-coal body away from me.

Joe   I bet Emile loved that.

Shanice   He weren't my boyfriend den.

Joe   And now?

Shanice   From den on, he loved to show how smart he was, like deh is two kinds of black, and he come from the better one, he was havin a laugh. People weren't gonna tek dat.

Joe   Including Emile?

Shanice   Why yu love to chat about Emile, yu love him?

Joe   It's just a question.

Shanice   Yu ask too many questions.

Joe   It's my job.

Shanice   So's listenin.

Joe   Aint I listening to you now?

Shanice   All dat shit in the paper, chattin like they knew him. He weren't special, he was juss anoder kid, he was nuttin.

Joe   So, he had it coming?

Shanice   I didn't say that.

Joe   So wat was he doing chatting to you about college?

Shanice   I dunno, he juss talked. I can't stop him from chattin.

Joe   But why you, Shanice?

Shanice   I dunno.

Joe   Maybe cos he thought the same way as your gran.

Shanice   Yer wastin yer time.

Joe   Why?

Shanice   Go back to ware yu come from.

Joe   This is where I come from.

Enter **Dwayne, Emile, Clinton** *and* **Perry**.

Dwayne   Tyson's soff.

Clinton   Awright, watch.

Dwayne   Wass he got, after my man Lennox give him a slappin?

Clinton   He's still a force.

Dwayne   He's a joke. He aint never bin the same since he come outta prison after wat dat gal said about him. He grind her, and wat happen, get banged up. Dat aint right.

Perry   My dad says, women are here to fuck up the black man.

Clinton   Yu don't even know yer dad.

Perry   Yer mama don't know yer dad.

Clinton   Dry!

Dwayne   Like her pussy.

Joe *laughs.*

Dwayne Awright, awright, who call the Feds?

Emile Was it yu, P?

Perry Yeah, I want dem to catch the bastard dat cut up Clinton's hair?

Clinton Ha, yer so funny.

Dwayne So wass my man doin here?

Shanice We're juss chattin, so leave him, yeah.

Dwayne Yu sexin him?

Shanice Oh man, juss step.

Dwayne Emile, have a word, man.

Shanice Excuse me, I'm right here.

Emile So ware's yer massa?

Shanice Emile?

Emile Ware him deh?

Clinton Cold.

Perry Gwan.

Emile Him let yu off the ball and chain fer the night? Him lose his tongue or wat?

Joe Toothpaste.

Emile Wass he say?

Clinton He said toothpaste.

Emile Yeah, I know wat he said.

Joe Well, you might want invest, ca yer breath stink, bredren.

Laughter.

Perry Oh shame!

Clinton   I knew he was gonna come out wid dat.

Dwayne   It's awright, Emile.

Emile   Get off.

Dwayne   Wat, yu go cryin to yer mummy now, ca the brudda here lick yu down wid sum lyrics?

Emile   He didn't lick me down.

Dwayne   And it was a dry one too.

Clinton   Toothpaste.

Emile   He aint no brudda.

Dwayne   Look like one to me.

Perry   Yu want invest in sum specs as well, Emile.

Clinton   As well as toothpaste.

Emile   Look at the fool.

Dwayne   Yeah?

Emile   Don't even know he's bin used.

Joe   Why don't you enlighten me?

Emile   We aint tellin yu shit.

Joe   So, you do know something?

Emile   No.

Joe   But you just told me you aint telling us shit.

Emile   See, awready I know wat yer doin.

Joe   I'm only repeating wat you said.

Emile   Yu go try twist my words, watch him now.

Joe   You're twisting your own words.

Shanice   Emile?

Emile   Is who ask yu fer anythin?

Joe   You said you aint telling us shit.

Emile   Yes.

Joe   Which implies, that you know something, but you refuse to share it with us.

Emile   No.

Joe   No, you refuse to share, or no, it isn't true?

Emile   See wat I mean about him?

Joe   You better watch yourself, Emile, that's a bad habit you picked up there.

Emile   Why don't yu juss go?

Dwayne   Shut up, yu fool.

Joe   Thank yu, Dwayne, control yer bwoi.

Clinton   Comin out wid dry lyrics himself now.

Joe   You had better keep a leash on this one, Dwayne. He may fold under questioning.

Dwayne   Sit down.

Joe   Bwoi.

Shanice   Why yu stressin him fer?

Perry   Rah, woman tougher than yu, Emile.

Shanice   Why don't yu juss go home?

Joe   I am home.

Dwayne   Wass dis?

Shanice   He say he comes from here.

Dwayne   Is it? Ware?

Joe   Dickens.

Dwayne   Knew it! Dat estate is soff!

Joe   Let me guess, Cleveland?

Perry   Believe.

Joe   Yu aint all dat.

Dwayne   Shut up, man.

Clinton   Wid yer dry chat.

Perry   Yu definitely aint bin back from time.

Joe   You Cleveland bwois are wurtless and you know it.

Dwayne   Talk to the hand.

Joe   Yu know it.

Dwayne   Dat was back in the day. Tings change.

Clinton   Believe.

Perry   Yeah.

Dwayne   Wat matters is now.

Joe   Awright, I'm down with that.

Dwayne   No yer not. Yu aint from round here no more, dread. So don't carry on like yu tink yu know.

Clinton   Chump.

Perry   If yer so bad, why yu leave fer?

Joe   I wanted a change. Cleaner air.

Emile   Well, gwan den, if dass how yu feel.

Joe   Yeah, but there's a little matter of a murder, Emile, remember?

Emile   Yu aint gonna find him here.

Joe   Maybe, maybe not.

Emile   Dis guy drive me mad.

Dwayne   Chill.

Emile   Juss say wat yu feel, yeah.

Joe   Your boy is losing it again, Dwayne, have a word.

Emile   Yu tink it's one of us, ennit?

Joe   You'll find out soon enough what I think.

Emile   Wass so special about dat bwoi anyhow? How many black bwois bin kill up round here?

Joe   That aint my business.

Emile   Course it aint. But Kwame was different, right. Ca he loved to act like a white man.

Clinton   Believe.

Joe   Whatever.

Emile   Go run back to yer slave masters.

Joe   Slave masters?

Emile   How yu know it weren't a white guy dat beat him?

Joe   I don't.

Emile   So wat yu doin here? A little bit of trouble.

Joe   A little bit?

Emile   And the first ting deh do is reach fer us. Always.

Joe   Oh look, don't gimme the 'police pick on us ca we're black' line. Ca I'd juss laugh in yer face. Why should people care about you, when you don't care about yourselves?

Emile   Ooh, man get vex.

Clinton   Oh yes.

Joe   Bwoi, you'll know when I get vex.

Emile   Is it?

Joe   You juss can't keep yer tail quiet, the lot of yer.

Dwayne   Awright, awright, let's juss chill now please, yeah. Peace. He don't speak fer the rest of us. Catch the rass dat did dis. Ennit, bwois?

Chorus of agreement.

Joe   I see.

Dwayne   Good. Dass good.

Joe   Don't go mistaking me for some other fool, yeah. Cos I aint leaving here till I catch somebody, and I will catch, trust. I'm gone. Shanice, always a pleasure.

Exit **Joe**.

Dwayne   Fool.

Clinton   He say he go catch sumone.

Dwayne   Catch wat? We supposed to be scared of dat?

Clinton   Nuh, man.

Perry   Safe.

Dwayne   And yu, lettin him get to yer.

Emile   I weren't.

Dwayne   He come like yer dad.

Emile   He don't look nuttin like my dad.

Dwayne   I didn't say he looked like yer dad, I said he come like yer dad, clean out yer ears. He's right, yu nuh, yer too touchy. No wonder my man's ridin yer arse. Hold it down, bwoi.

Emile   I was.

Dwayne   Yu want get catch?

Shanice   Leave him.

Dwayne   Gal, shut up, I'm juss tryin to stop my bwoi here from goin to prison, yeah.

Shanice   And yerself.

Dwayne   Yu want control yer woman please?

Shanice   Yu gonna let him speak to me like dat, Emile?

Dwayne   Emile!

Emile   Leave me!

Shanice   Oh man.

Emile   Every time yu two start, it's me in the middle. Yu want fight, gwan.

Exit **Emile**.

Dwayne   Bring dat fool back.

Shanice   Let him sulk.

Dwayne   Gwan.

Exit **Perry** *and* **Clinton**.

Shanice   Wat am I doin?

Dwayne   Yu gonna cook me sum food?

Shanice   No.

Dwayne   Rude!

Shanice   Wat yu want?

Dwayne   Number two.

Shanice   Wat yu starin at?

Dwayne   Nuttin.

Shanice   I'm up here, yu know. Perv man. 'Bout yu lookin down my top.

Dwayne   I weren't.

Shanice   I saw yu.

Dwayne   Yu look nicer in dat oder top. Put it on.

Shanice   I don't have it.

Dwayne   Get anoder one. I'll pay fer it.

Shanice   Dry.

Dwayne   I chat better than Emile. Wat yu doin wid him?

Shanice   Who, yer best friend? I love him.

Dwayne (*sucks his teeth*)   Yer juss lookin after him. Like yu look after troll.

Shanice   Don't call her dat.

Dwayne   Shut up.

Shanice   Yu know she fancies yer.

Dwayne   Who's lookin after yu? When yu go have sum fun?

Shanice   Yu think I want fun wid yu?

Dwayne   Don't yu get bored?

Shanice   I'm gettin bored right now.

Dwayne   Come on.

Shanice   Don't touch me.

Dwayne   Yer lucky dass all I'm doin. Nuff brers round here want ride yu, yu nuh.

Shanice   Yu on crack?

Dwayne   How yu gonna fight dem all off? Dass how bad it's gettin. Yu don't know wat yer doin, yu got no idea. The fact dat yer goin wid sum fool, mek dem want it even more. I keep tellin dem nuff times, no one touches yu, but I can't hold dem off for ever, Shanice.

Shanice   Yu couldn't hold yerself.

Dwayne   Yu wanted it dat night.

Shanice   I was drunk.

Dwayne   Yu were sexed up. Yu know if one a dem so much as looks at yu funny, I'd kill dem.

Shanice   How nice.

Dwayne   Yer so fit. Wat? Yu rather I chat rubbish to yu?

Shanice   Go on den, try.

Dwayne   Move.

Shanice   Deh's no one else here. Come on, I want to see dis. Try. Come on. Fer me.

Beat.

Dwayne   I love yer hands, yu got nice hands.

Shanice *laughs.*

Dwayne   Yu want die?

Shanice   Yu are so sad. Yu run Emile down day and night, den yu have nerve to steal his lines. Sad!

Dwayne   Move.

Shanice   But oder than dat, not bad, I'd have to think about it.

Dwayne   Yu know wat else I can't get over. Seein yu, yer first day at school, I thought, Rah!, dat can't be the same Shanice Roberts who I used to live next door to, went primary school wid. Wid yer pigtails, and her nappy head. Playin football wid me.

Shanice   I whopped yer arse at football. Remember dat five-a-side tournament?

Dwayne   Yu score a couple of goals and yu think yer it.

Shanice   Three.

Dwayne   Dat third one was not a goal.

Shanice   Deh yu go.

Dwayne   It weren't.

Shanice   Oh Dwayne man, it was seven years ago.

Dwayne   It weren't a goal.

Shanice Give it up.

Dwayne I can't stop thinkin about yu.

Shanice Dwayne, please.

Dwayne Yer hauntin me, yu know dat?

Shanice *laughs.*

Dwayne Don't laugh at me.

Shanice Yu want have yerself a cold shower, dread.

Dwayne Yu carry on.

Shanice I will.

Dwayne Yer gonna get hurt, yer gonna get hurt bad! Wass dat fool Emile gonna do den?

Shanice He wouldn't be if he stopped mixin wid yu.

Dwayne Is it my fault he keeps reachin out to me?

Shanice I'm the one dass holdin him when he has his nightmares.

Dwayne Is it? Ware?

Shanice Yer nasty.

Dwayne Chill.

Shanice 'Kick him in the head, kick him.'

Dwayne I didn't tell him.

Shanice Yu made him.

Dwayne No, Shanice, yu made him. Yu told him Kwame was sexin yu. Sorry, yeah.

Shanice Don't touch me.

Dwayne Shanice.

Shanice Go brush yer teeth.

Dwayne Yu go free it up soon, yu know it.

Shanice   Not fer yu.

Dwayne   I hope they rape yu up bad.

Enter **Ronnie**.

Ronnie   Got yer change. Yu know how far I had to go. Awright, Dwayne?

Dwayne   Troll.

Exit **Dwayne**.

Shanice   Gimme my change.

Ronnie *throws money to the ground.*

Shanice   Oh Ronnie.

Exit **Ronnie**.

Shanice   Yeah, gwan, run!

Exit **Shanice**.

Enter **Joe** *and* **Matt**.

Joe   See that basketball court.

Matt   You are changing the subject.

Joe   That is where the old huts used to be, for the dustbins.

Matt   Really?

Joe   I had a girl in there once.

Matt   I beg your pardon?

Joe   I was fifteen. Mandy Cook, oh man, she was fine. Huts were the only place we could go to. Mandy Cook. First white girl I had, you know. Tellin you, she was . . .

Matt   Fit, thank you.

Joe   Just trying to lighten the mood.

Matt   Look, Joe, I know you haven't been with us for long.

Joe   Uh-huh?

Matt   So you might not be up to speed with how we do things here.

Joe   Probably not.

Matt   I'd appreciate it if you did not go off on your own. We work together.

Joe   Of course.

Matt   We follow our lines of inquiry together.

Joe   Absolutely.

Matt   So we understand each other?

Joe   Of course, Matt.

Matt   Good.

Joe   The thing is though.

Matt   Yes?

Joe   The girl knows something.

Matt   Did you think you could charm it out of her?

Joe   Well, we don't have much else.

Matt   I'm aware of that.

Joe   Haven't you noticed, everything's scaling down?

Matt   I'm aware of that as well.

Joe   It's not news any more. Soon, he'll just be another dead black kid. Kids round here aren't made to feel important. They never have. They know a token gesture when they see it.

Matt   I was beginning to think you didn't care.

Joe   I don't. (*Beat.*) I want to know what he was doing in there.

Matt   Ordering food.

Joe   So she said. But he never came out wid any.

Matt   He was eating in.

Joe   For ten minutes? Counting the five or six it takes to cook. I was thinking, maybe he was buying drugs there.

Matt   Joe, can I ask you something?

Joe   Just tell me, don't ask.

Matt   Why are you so eager to demean him?

Joe   Oh man.

Matt   He was a bright young lad. Four weeks away from starting university, he had a future, he didn't deserve to die like that.

Joe   You trying to impress me, Matt?

Matt   With what?

Joe   What a cool liberal you are.

Matt   Meaning?

Joe   Meaning that. I mean, come on, it's really got to get to you, all this PC shit.

Matt   Not particularly.

Joe   Not even a little?

Matt   The Met needs to change. We can't keep making mistakes.

Joe   It's the uniforms I feel sorry for. Now they're thinking of asking them to provide written records for every stop and search. I mean, what kind of stupidness is that?

Matt *sighs.*

Joe   What? What is it?

Matt   I don't understand you.

Joe   Good.

Matt   Joe, if you have a problem working with me on this case . . .

Joe   What case? We both know why I'm here. It's bring out the poster boy. Make the Met look good. McPherson report. Well, that's fine, but you had better step back, boy, and let me do my job.

Matt   First off, I am not your boy. Second, I am the senior officer.

Joe   Yes! Go, Matt! Stand yer ground, don't take shit from anybody.

Matt   Please, don't patronise me.

Joe   Ditto.

Matt   I was not.

Joe   It's always going to be in our job, prejudice.

Matt   I am not prejudiced.

Joe   Easy, Matt, it's only a word, you don't have to shit yourself.

Matt   I'm not. Alright?

Joe   If you're walking down the street at night, you see a bunch of black lads walking towards you . . .

Matt   Oh, come on.

Joe   . . . You know you're gonna cross that road, as fast as your legs can tek you. You know! It's all preconceived. Maybe this Kwame was a good kid, I don't know.

Matt   He was.

Joe   But he's from that estate. We've got to find out if he's a bad boy. We have to ask those questions, and I don't care.

Matt   That doesn't make it right.

Joe   It's the way it is.

Exit **Joe** *and* **Matt**.

Enter **Shanice** *and* **Emile**.

Emile   Rape yer!

Shanice   Dass wat the bastard said.

Emile   Wat yu mean rape?

Shanice   Wat yu think I mean? The bwoi nasty, dass wat I keep tellin yu.

Emile   Like he meant it?

Shanice   Whether he meant it or not, it was a nasty ting to say, don't yu think? Emile?

Emile   I don't blasted know.

Shanice   Yu don't know?

Emile   Wat yu stressin me fer?

Shanice   It's not a hard thing to work out, Emile. Was he right or wrong to say it?

Emile   He was wrong.

Shanice   Don't strain yerself.

Emile   I said he was wrong, wat yu want?

Shanice   Deal wid it.

Emile   I'm aways dealin wid it.

Shanice   Talk to him.

Emile   Yu mad?

Shanice   Tell him I'm yer gal, tell him he can't treat me like dis.

Emile   Awright!

Shanice   Why yu so soff?

Emile   Yu gonna dog me out now?

Shanice   No.

Emile   Lie.

Shanice   I want things the way they were.

Emile   Go college like Clinton?

Shanice   Yes.

Emile   Gal, dat aint fer us, Miss Douglas took care of dat.

Shanice   Don't worry yerself about her.

Emile   Maybe yu should.

Shanice   Should wat?

Emile   Fuck him. Fuck him, Shanice. One time, yeah.

Shanice   No, yu did not say dat.

Emile   Dwayne's right, yeah, yu don't know wat yer doin, wat yer givin out. I can't tek it, man. Whenever my back's turned, wonderin all the time if Dwayne or anyone else is sexin yu. It's drivin me mad, not knowin, so juss fuck him, yeah. Least I'll know, I'll have sum peace, I'll forgive yu, we'll move on.

Shanice *screams. Attacks* **Emile**.

Emile   I'm sorry, I'm sorry!!

Shanice   Yu love doin dis to me or wat?

Emile   I don't know wat I'm doin, yeah.

Shanice   It's aways about yu.

Emile   I keep seein his . . .

Shanice   . . . his face, yeah!

Emile   I'll talk to Dwayne.

Shanice   Don't worry yerself.

Emile   I said I'll talk to him. Don't leave me.

Exit **Emile**.

Enter **Ronnie**.

Shanice Yu sure dis is the right road?

Ronnie Yes.

Shanice Ashwood Gardens?

Ronnie Yes.

Shanice Not Ashwood Square?

Ronnie No.

Shanice Twenty-nine C?

Ronnie Yes.

Shanice Are yu gonna say more than word to me tonight?

Ronnie No.

Shanice Bet yu do.

Ronnie Bet I don't.

Shanice (*laughs*) See!

Ronnie Oh, juss leave me.

Shanice Yer soff, Ronnie. Ronnie?

Ronnie Get off me, don't do dat, Shanice. Move!

Shanice Oh, so yu want fight me now?

Ronnie Kick yer arse. It's big enuff.

Shanice *grabs her, holds her playfully in a headlock.*

Ronnie Get off.

Shanice Say it.

Ronnie Get off me.

Shanice Say it!

Ronnie Yer arse aint big.

Shanice Better.

Ronnie It's Jurassic!

Shanice *grabs her again.*

Ronnie Awright!

Shanice (*backs off*) Well, gimme a smile den.

Ronnie I don't feel like smilin.

Shanice Oh Ronnie.

Ronnie Don't Ronnie me.

Shanice Come here and gimme a hug. Come here.

Ronnie I don't hug hos.

Shanice Excuse me?

Ronnie Yer a ho.

Shanice Listen, I'm gonna say dis one lass time, yeah, deh is nuttin goin on between . . .

Ronnie . . . between me and Dwayne!

Shanice So yu think yer funny now?

Ronnie Yer a liar.

Shanice I aint lyin to yu, Ronnie.

Ronnie Yu lied to me before, den I had to find out from Clinton, yu were grindin Dwayne.

Shanice Once, I grind him once.

Ronnie Yu still lied dough.

Shanice Only cos I know how yu go all menstrual when it comes to Dwayne.

Ronnie Yu love to do dis to me.

Shanice Yu know wat, yu can fuck off, yeah.

Ronnie   Wat?

Shanice   Fuck off. Move. Now.

Ronnie   Wass up wid yu?

Shanice   Yu! Yer so jealous.

Ronnie   Yu got everythin.

Shanice   I got nuttin but grief.

Ronnie   Yu got Dwayne droolin.

Shanice   I don't know wat yu see in de fool, I really don't.

Ronnie   He likes yu.

Shanice   So?

Ronnie   Why can't I be yu?

Shanice   Yu not turnin lesbian on me?

Ronnie   Move.

Shanice   Dat I don't need.

Ronnie   I said no.

Shanice   Look at me. I said look. (*Beat.*) Don't chat fuck ries in my face again, yu understand?

Ronnie   Yes.

Shanice   Don't be me, Ronnie. It's overrated.

Ronnie   I won't den.

Shanice   We awright?

Ronnie   Yeah.

Shanice   Yu sure?

Ronnie   Yeah.

Shanice   Cool.

Ronnie   She's comin.

Shanice   Right.

Enter **Miss Douglas**.

Awright?

Miss Douglas   Yes, thank you.

Shanice   Yu got a light?

Miss Douglas   I don't smoke.

Ronnie   She don't recognise us.

Miss Douglas   That's not true.

Shanice   See, yu get Ronnie all upset now.

Miss Douglas   Then I apologise.

Shanice   Aint yu gonna say hello?

Miss Douglas   Hello, Shanice.

Shanice   Hello, Miss.

Ronnie   I love yer house, Miss. Nice.

Miss Douglas   Thank you.

Shanice   Ware yu goin?

Miss Douglas   I'd like to go home.

Shanice   Stay and chat.

Ronnie   Yeah, stay and chat.

Shanice   Yu bin shoppin, Miss?

Miss Douglas   Yes.

Shanice   Let me see.

Miss Douglas (*pleads*)   Please.

Shanice   Please wat?

Ronnie   Aint even touched her yet, and she's sweatin awready.

Miss Douglas   What do you want?

Shanice   To chat.

Ronnie   Yu deaf?

Shanice   So how's it goin, Miss?

Miss Douglas   Fine.

Shanice   How's school?

Miss Douglas   Fine.

Shanice   Yu miss us?

Ronnie   Do yu miss us?

Shanice   Course she does, Ronnie, check her face.

Ronnie   She's sorry.

Shanice   Is dat true, Miss, yu sorry?

Miss Douglas   Yes, I am sorry.

Shanice   Yu lie bad.

Ronnie   She'd say yes to anythin, to get away.

Shanice   Believe.

Ronnie   Yu a prostitute, Miss? Say yes.

Miss Douglas   I don't know what it is you want.

Shanice   To chat.

Ronnie   Still deaf.

Miss Douglas   Please don't do this.

Shanice   Don't do wat, Miss?

Miss Douglas   You are only making things worse for yourself.

Shanice   Is it?

Miss Douglas   Let me pass.

Ronnie   Yu don't tell us wat to do no more.

Shanice   Nice watch. Take it off.

Miss Douglas (*removes watch*)   May I go now?

Ronnie   Yu know, I'd shut up if I were yu.

Miss Douglas   You have not changed at all.

Shanice   Don't chat to her like dat. We're out here now.

Ronnie   Believe.

Shanice   Dis is our school.

Miss Douglas   Look, I will not be intimidated like this.

Shanice   Is it?

Ronnie   Can hear her heart pumpin from here.

Miss Douglas   I won't allow it.

Shanice   Yu won't allow it?

Ronnie   Gonna put us in detention? Miss tink she bad now.

Miss Douglas   You cannot keep doing this, blaming everyone else for your mistakes.

Shanice   Wat have I said about talkin like dat? 'bout yu darkin us?

Miss Douglas   You stole Mr Ferns's wallet, girl.

Shanice   I was puttin it back.

Miss Douglas   Oh come on.

Shanice   I was.

Ronnie   Yu were puttin it back?

Shanice   Quiet.

Miss Douglas   We have been through this.

Shanice   We go thru it again.

Miss Douglas   I caught you red-handed.

Shanice   Yu caught me puttin it back.

Ronnie   Yu soff.

Shanice   Shut up.

Miss Douglas   You had his money in your pocket, explain that to me.

Shanice   I don't have to explain shit.

Miss Douglas   Oh Shanice?

Shanice   Step!!

Ronnie   Wat yu tryin to touch her fer? Yu a dyke, Miss?

Miss Douglas   Listen to me.

Shanice   Couldn't wait, man, yu wanted me outta deh.

Miss Douglas   You know that isn't true.

Shanice   And den yu had to start on Emile.

Miss Douglas   He threw a chair at me.

Ronnie   Did yu like wat I did, Miss?

Miss Douglas   Oh yes, Veronica, you trashing my car was a nice touch.

Ronnie   Cool. Gimme yer money.

Miss Douglas   Shanice, please listen to me.

Ronnie   Gimme it.

Miss Douglas   Why are you still letting yourself get led around by her?

Ronnie   She is dead.

Shanice   Hold it down.

Ronnie   Nuh, man.

Shanice   Hold it down, Ronnie.

Ronnie   Shanice!

Shanice   Go stand over deh. Go. Yu betrayed me.

Miss Douglas   What is it you think you did to me?

Shanice   It's all yer fault.

Miss Douglas   All I ever did was try and help you. I had no choice.

Shanice   It was juss a wallet, man.

Miss Douglas   It was wrong.

Shanice   I was puttin it back, yu deaf?

Miss Douglas   It was too late. You came so far, you were doing so well.

Shanice   So why open yer mout den?

Miss Douglas   Why did you take it?

Shanice   I dunno, I juss did.

Miss Douglas   Was it her?

Shanice   Leave her.

Miss Douglas   Did she put you up to it?

Ronnie   Wass she say?

Miss Douglas   When are you going to learn, Shanice, people like her don't want to be helped? They don't want to listen.

Shanice   I am people like her.

Miss Douglas   No, you are not. You're just scared.

Shanice   Don't play me. I wasted nuff times listenin to yu, and I still got fling out.

Ronnie   I'm bored now, man, do her, den let's go.

Shanice   Hand over yer money.

Miss Douglas   No.

Shanice   Miss!

Miss Douglas   I will not. You won't hurt me.

Shanice   I will.

Miss Douglas   No, you won't.

Shanice   I will.

Ronnie   Juss do it.

Miss Douglas   Stay out of this, Veronica.

Ronnie   Stop callin me dat.

Miss Douglas   Still thinking a foul mouth is going to get you everything you want.

Ronnie   Let's juss tek her money and go, Shanice man.

Shanice   I want her to gimme it.

Miss Douglas   You are going to have to take it.

Shanice   Gimme it.

Miss Douglas   No.

Ronnie   Shanice!

Shanice   Leave me!

Miss Douglas   Why couldn't you leave her alone?

Ronnie   She renk!

Miss Douglas   You are nothing, Veronica Davis, you always were.

Ronnie   Yu gonna let her chat like dat?

Miss Douglas   Please, Shanice.

Ronnie   Yu think yu be sellin burgers if yu didn't get fling out?

Miss Douglas   Listen to me.

Ronnie   Wid yer shit money every month, hair smellin of onion.

Miss Douglas   Shanice?

Ronnie   Every night, dread.

Miss Douglas (*pleads*)   Please.

Ronnie   Do her!

Shanice *strikes her.*

Ronnie   Oh! Shame! I felt dat from here. Tek her money and let's go.

Shanice   Yu happy now?

Ronnie   Shanice!

Shanice   Yu happy?

Ronnie   Wat yu goin on wid?

Shanice   Are yu?

Ronnie   Come on!

Exit **Shanice**.

Ronnie   Ware yu goin? (*To* **Miss Douglas**.) Ware yu goin? Money.

Miss Douglas   I knew you'd end up like this.

Ronnie   Is my name Shanice? I don't business wat yu think of me, yeah. I know yer scared. Believe.

Exit **Ronnie** *and* **Miss Douglas**.

Enter **Dwayne**.

Dwayne   I'm here. Come on!

Enter **Emile**.

Dwayne (*laughs*)   Wat?

Emile   Bastard man.

Dwayne Shut yer noise.

Emile Yer a bastard, Dwayne. Leavin me like dat.

Dwayne Is it my fault yu can't run?

Emile I know how to run, I can run faster than yu.

Dwayne So wat happened? Yu go cry?

Emile Shoulda told me yu weren't payin him.

Dwayne We done it before.

Emile Still shoulda said. Coulda bin prepared.

Dwayne Bwoi love to moan.

Emile Guy nearly caught me.

Dwayne I bet he's still lookin.

Emile I bet he calls the police.

Dwayne Hey, it's me who should be callin. 'bout he charge us ten squid from town. Teif! Hear how the controller said it would be seven or summin. But my man deh try and shake us fer ten. Hear how he spoke. 'Ware yu goin, boss, ten pound, boss.' Stupid Arab. Should tell him about him claart! Go back to Iraq! See how long his beard was? Bin Laden's brudda. Yu know how many bruddas dat man's got? Untold! His mama's hole muss be dat big.

Emile Aint his mum. His dad have a whole heap of women.

Dwayne Must be a bro. Gimme a draw. Bloody cheer up, man, wass up wid yu?

Emile Juss don't leave me like dat again.

Dwayne Yeah, wass yer wurtless rass gonna do?

Emile I aint no rass.

Dwayne Rass.

Emile Don't call me dat.

Dwayne   Rass! Yu still comin out wid nish, Emile, wat yu gonna do?

Emile   Yu'll find out.

Dwayne   Chill. Before I slap yu.

Emile   Juss tell me wat yer doin.

Dwayne   I'm tellin yu to chill. Hey, don't step up, unless yu gonna jump.

Emile   Yer mad.

Dwayne   Is it?

Emile   Outta control, dread.

Dwayne   Me?

Emile   Yu didn't have to hit the guy.

Dwayne   He ask fer it.

Emile   Six times? Have a heart, blood.

Dwayne   Like yu had fer Kwame?

Emile   He deserved it.

Dwayne   So yu tink yer bad now?

Emile   I want respect.

Dwayne   Wat yu goin on wid?

Emile   Shanice said . . .

Dwayne   Shanice? Don't come to me wid shit from yer gal, 'bout Shanice!

Emile   Yu still don't respect me, do yer?

Dwayne   Yer chattin like a spas.

Emile   I did wat yu all wanted.

Dwayne   Yu don't want to start dis wid me.

Emile   I want respect, I want it now, bredren.

Dwayne   Well, yu aint gonna get it.

Emile   Yu love to put me down.

Dwayne   Yer too soff.

Emile   I've had enuff.

Dwayne   Is it?

Emile   Wat more I have to do?

Dwayne   Yer soff!

Emile   And stop tryin to sex Shanice, she's my woman.

Dwayne   I'll sex who I like, bwoi!

Emile   Yu aint.

Dwayne   Yu really are stupid, ennit? Dat policeman know it too.

Emile   Leave her alone, Dwayne.

Dwayne   Watch me stroke her leg, every time yer deh. Watch me run my train up her arse, watch me. Yu might learn summin. I'm gonna run it good, man, gonna run it. And yu aint gonna do nuttin, ca yer soff.

Emile *pulls out his blade, aims it at* **Dwayne***'s face.*

Dwayne   Yeah? Wat? Wat?

Emile   Yu see it?

Dwayne   Yu tink I'm blind?

Emile   I buy dis fer yu.

Dwayne   Yu pull it, yu best use it.

Emile   I will.

Dwayne   Wat she see in yu?

Emile   She my woman. And I want respect!

Dwayne   (*laughs*) Yu.

Emile   Idiot? Fool? Arsehole? Who's soff now? Who's soff now?

Dwayne   Me?

Emile   Who have the blade?

Dwayne   Yu.

Emile   Yu know who yu look like, Dwayne? Like one a dem white cunts who clutch their bags warever we see dem.

Sound of police sirens.

Dwayne   Yu hear dat?

Emile   Yu a white cunt, Dwayne?

Dwayne   Dass the cab driver tellin dem about us, we gotta go.

Emile   Are yu a white cunt?

Dwayne   Yeah.

Emile   Believe.

Exit **Dwayne**.

Enter **Joe**.

Joe   Bwoi, Emile! You know how to run fast, man! Look at me, I have no breath left. You alright? Take deep breaths, my man.

Emile   Move.

Joe   Alright.

Emile   Yer lucky I trip up.

Joe   Yeah.

Emile   No way could yu catch me.

Joe   I almost had you.

Emile   Yu want go again?

Joe   You mad?

Emile   Yer soff.

Joe   I bet you used to run for your school? Am I right?

Emile   Yeah.

Joe   Medals and shit?

Emile   Untold.

Joe   Me too.

Emile   Yu?

Joe   What, you don't believe?

Emile   Yer outta shape, blood.

Joe   That was then, this is now.

Emile   Believe.

Joe   So what happened to you, Emile? Didn't you want to be an athlete? Why aren't you running now?

Emile   Dunno.

Joe   Don't chat like you're an idiot.

Emile   Move.

Joe   What happened?

Emile   I dunno. Shit, shit 'appens.

Joe   Like what? What shit? Tell me what happened to you.

Emile   Yu tink I want tell yu?

Joe   Fine. Stay stupid.

Emile   So wat about yu?

Joe   Me?

Emile   Dickens, bwoi. Wat 'appen to yu? Didn't yu want to be a policeman?

Joe   Are you cussing me?

Emile   Yeah, I'm cussin yu.

Joe   Lose the tone, Emile. Have some respect.

Emile   Yer not my dad.

Joe (*laughs*)   Look, just tell me what you were running from just then?

Emile   Heard the sirens.

Joe   Yeah, so what you running for? What's your naughty little black arse been up to now, Emile? What you do?

Emile   Nuttin.

Joe   You're a bad liar.

Emile   Is it?

Joe   People who run have something to hide.

Emile   Is it?

Joe   Yes it is.

Emile   People also run ca they don't like gettin stressed by all yer friends, ennit? I aint got time fer dat.

Joe   You? Where the hell you going, work? (*Laughs.*) I was lookin for yu, I want to chat to you.

Emile   I don't wanna chat to yu.

Joe   Now you're hurtin my feelins.

Emile   Is it?

Joe   I was hoping we could spend some quality time together.

Emile   Wat yu tink I am?

Joe   Come, stand up.

Emile   Ware we goin?

Joe   Take a guess.

Enter **Matt**.

Joe   So, Emile, the guy on your left is your boy Clinton, and over there, we have Perry, and that has got to be Dwayne, right here, see that boy there, you see him?

Emile   I aint blind.

Joe   That's Kwame.

Emile   I know.

Matt   You know?

Emile   Yeah. I know. I went school wid him.

Joe   Well that's good, because you're going to recognise this young fella right here. That's you.

Emile   That aint me.

Joe   Hold up a second, I've got a better picture here. It really gets your face. You wouldn't believe the trouble we went through to get these pictures.

Emile   Is it?

Joe   Trust. Here we are. See it there?

Emile   Yeah. Aint me.

Joe   That's not you?

Emile   Aint me.

Joe   Well, that's a big relief.

Emile   Yeah?

Joe   Yes, cos then, if that was you, and your friends, at this particular place, at this particular time, with Kwame, approximately five minutes before he died, then you and your friends would have some serious explaining to do, me and my friend here, wouldn't have to reach for a search warrant, knock on your mother's door, you still live at

home, course you do, go through all her things, same thing
with your friends, bring them all in here, one by one, see
what they say, find out if they are a bigger jackass than you.
But like you said, dat aint you.

Emile Can I go now?

Joe Sit down.

Emile Yu can bring in who yu like. Deh won't say nuttin.

Joe Say what? What aren't they going to say?

Emile Nuttin.

Joe So, they do know something?

Emile Don't play me, yeah.

Joe Play you with what?

Emile Wid dem words.

Joe Are you stupid?

Matt Joe?

Emile Yeah, tell yer bwoi to chill.

Matt Why don't you stop wasting our time.

Emile I'm juss messin wid yu.

Matt Tell us about these.

Joe You're all laughing in this one, what's that about?

Emile Nuttin to say. We're juss laughin about, havin a
laugh.

Joe Did you kill Kwame for a laugh?

Emile No.

Joe So why did you kill him?

Emile I didn't.

Joe You know who did?

Emile   No.

Joe   This picture was taken five minutes before he was beaten up, Emile.

Emile   And yer point is?

Joe   You are probably the last ones to see him.

Emile   Yer point?

Joe   And you don't know anything?

Emile   Is wat I said.

Joe   Alright. So tell me something you do know. What was the conversation about. (*Holds up photo.*) Tell me. What were you laughing about?

Emile   Can't remember.

Joe   Try.

Emile   I was tellin a joke.

Joe   A joke?

Emile   Yeah.

Joe   Must have been a good joke.

Emile   It was.

Joe   Well, let's hear it then. The joke.

Emile   Yer soff.

Joe   And you're a liar.

Emile   Wat do yu call a lesbian dinosaur?

Joe   I give up.

Emile   A lickalottapus.

Joe   That's it?

Emile   Yes.

Joe   Weren't that funny.

Emile   Yeah, well, dass yu.

Joe   That was the same joke you told Kwame?

Emile   It's wat I said.

Joe   But it isn't funny. Ignorant, yeah, but not funny.

Emile   We laughed.

Joe   I don't see Kwame laughing.

Emile   Well, he was.

Joe   It looks he's crying.

Emile   He weren't cryin.

Joe   Like he's scared. What has he got to be scared about?

Emile   Yu tell me.

Joe   You threaten him?

Emile   No.

Joe   What did you do to him?

Emile   Nuttin. We pass him by the street, told the joke, and we left him.

Joe   You left him there to die.

Emile   No.

Joe   Yes.

Emile   We juss left him.

Joe   Did you like him?

Emile   He was awright.

Joe   Why?

Emile   Wass dis fool sayin now?

Joe   Why did you like him? He was nothing but a bookworm, a nerd, a little fool. What was he going do with his life? Go to university, get a nice job, forty grand a year, you think? He was heading out of the estate for good. Then, there's you. Dashed out of school at fifteen. What have you got in common with him? How could you be friends with him?

Emile   Did I say we were friends?

Joe   Alright, now we're heading somewhere.

Emile   I said I liked him.

Joe   Are you a battyman, Emile?

Matt   Joe!

Emile   Yer the battyman.

Joe   You liked him? That Zulu warrior, who's as black as coal? Who thought he was smarter than the lot of you?

Emile   Yer words, dread.

Joe   You liked him?

Emile   Yeah.

Joe   Does Dwayne know you're this soft?

Emile   I aint soff.

Joe   He was a nice-looking boy though.

Emile   Yu are a battyman.

Joe   He must have had a lot of girls reaching for him.

Emile   Yeah?

Joe   Him and Shanice would've made a nice couple, don't you think, if she wasn't going out with you, that is.

Emile   She is goin out wid me.

Joe   I know. But if she weren't. Did he step to your woman, Emile, is that how it was? You aint having that, some bwoi tryin to grind your woman. I wouldn't have that. Is that what occurred, Emile? Is that what occurred?

Emile   No.

Joe   You can talk to me.

Emile   I am talkin.

Joe   See, what I can't figure out, what I can't get my head round, is this. This picture. You and your friends, other end of the high street, laughing your heads off, look at the time, five minutes after Kwame was found in the street, with his head cracked open. You lot, laughing like it didn't mean a thing.

Emile   Ca we didn't know.

Joe   Tell me.

Emile   I am.

Joe   Tell me what happened. We all get a little upset.

Emile   I aint upset.

Joe   Especially over a woman. I know how it goes, come on, Emile, bend my ear, bro to bro.

Emile   I aint yer bro. I aint yer nuttin. Yu love to tink yer down wid us.

Matt   Alright.

Emile   Yer nuttin to me.

Matt   Sit down, Emile.

Emile   So don't come it, yeah, don't play the big man.

Matt   Sit down please.

Emile   Well, tell yer bitch to chill den. Ca' dass all yu are now, dis fool's bitch! And I aint growin up to be no white man's bitch, yu get me?

Joe   You don't like bitches, do you, Emile?

Emile   No.

Joe   Was Kwame a bitch?

Emile   Yes.

Joe   Is that why you killed him?

Emile   No.

Joe   So why did you kill him?

Emile   I didn't.

Joe   You couldn't stand it.

Emile   I don't talk to yu.

Joe   He was a reminder.

Emile   I'd rather chat to him.

Joe   Of what a wurtless, useless rass you are.

Matt   Let's take a break.

Joe   Ennit, Emile?

Matt   Interview suspended at 16.10 p.m.

Exit **Emile**.

Matt   I'm releasing him.

Joe   Are you mad?

Matt   We're going round in circles in there. We've got nothing to charge him with. You need to calm down.

Joe   For fuck's sake.

Matt   Will you please calm down.

Joe   Facety little nigger.

Matt   Joe?

Joe   You want to see yourself, eyes as big as saucers. Yes, Matt, I said nigger. Do you want say it, go on, give it a try, let it out. Cos if I'm thinking it, so are you. Nigger!

Matt   Stop it.

Joe   Little shit.

Matt   Are you done?

Joe   Boy wanna learn respect.

Matt   Calm down, please.

Joe   Oh, will you stop saying please, it drive me mad! He did it. I know he did it. You know he did it. Bwoi thinks he's bad, him and his crew. I'll show dem who's bad. Aint nuttin but a low-life useless cold-blooded black bastard. He thinks he's summin, he aint nuttin. I'm havin him.

Matt   With what exactly? You've got nothing.

Joe   Don't butt in like that again.

Matt   I'm sorry?

Joe   Mek me look bad.

Matt   You were losing it.

Joe   It was working.

Matt   He wanted to talk to me more than you.

Joe   Love to hold his hand.

Matt   Your way wasn't working.

Joe (*laughs*)   Fool don't even know he's bin insulted.

Matt   Don't push your luck.

Joe   You do nish for one black kid, too much for the other one.

Matt   Oh that's right, go there.

Joe   You all think you're doing them a favour by patronising them.

Matt   I wasn't patronising him. Look, I do not wish to fight you, Joe.

Joe   Why? What you so bloody 'fraid to say, man?

Matt   Hold it down.

Joe   I don't want to hold it down. I want to talk. I want us to talk. I want us to have the conversation. Yeah? So let's have it.

Matt   I'm releasing him.

Exit **Joe** *and* **Matt**.

Enter **Shanice**, **Ronnie**, **Perry**, **Emile**, **Clinton** *and* **Dwayne**.

Shanice   Perry, dat had better not be spliff yer smokin.

Perry   Nuh, man.

Shanice   Wat have I told yu, not in here.

Perry   Shut up and gimme my fries.

Shanice   Who yu tellin to shut up? Yu mad?

Perry   Emile?

Emile   Chill.

Shanice   Dat had better be him yer sayin dat to.

Perry   Emile?

Shanice   Emile!

Emile   Yer shamin me, Shanice.

Perry   Thank yu.

Ronnie   Yu shame yerself.

Perry   Yu gonna take dat?

Emile   Shut yer mout.

Perry   Oh right, so bwoi tink he man now.

Emile   I don't think, I know.

Perry   Dwayne, put dis fool under manners again fer me please.

Emile   Why don't yu?

Perry   Awright den, come.

Dwayne   Sit down.

Perry   Yu fight like a gal anyhow.

Emile   Is it?

Perry   Believe.

Dwayne   Put out the spliff.

Perry   Dwayne man.

Dwayne   Yer fuckin up my sinuses wid dat, put it out.

Clinton   Are we all done now? Can we divvy up now please?

Clinton *produces a handbag, the boys rifle through it.*

Perry   See dat woman's face? See how scared? Feel my heart.

Clinton   Move.

Perry   Feel it, dread.

Clinton   Like a drum.

Perry   Better than weed.

Emile   Better than speed.

Clinton   Better than a line.

Perry   Yu tek line?

Clinton   Yes.

Perry   Since when?

Clinton   A boy at college had sum.

Perry   I thought I tell yu to stay away from dat?

Clinton   Step off P.

Perry   I'm telling yer mum, yu get dis (*Raises his hand.*).

Emile   Yu got the rest of the money in yer pocket deh, Dwayne?

Dwayne   Wat?

Emile   Rest of the money, dread.

Dwayne   Rest of the money here.

Emile   Nuh, man. I saw yu open the purse, deh was more deh.

Dwayne   Is it?

Emile   Yer holdin out on us, bro. Come on, man, cough up the rest, aint got all night.

Dwayne   Deh is no more.

Emile   Right now, on the table, if yu please.

Perry   Emile, yu mad or wat?

Dwayne   I'm tellin yu now, Emile, dis was all the money dat was in dat bag.

Emile   Well, yu mus be high from Perry's weed den, ca I definitely saw more dough in dat purse. Now I know yu don't wanna skank us, so wa gwan? Yer dad still fleecin yu or wat?

Dwayne   Don't do dis. Awright? Yu understand?

Emile   Awright, blood, ease up.

Dwayne   Yu ease up.

Emile   I'm cool. Keep the money.

Dwayne   Deh's no more money.

Emile   Awright, man, watever, I made a mistake den.

Dwayne   Yer damn right.

Exit **Dwayne**.

Emile   Oh come on, Dwayne!

Clinton   Yu are well and truly mad, yu nuh.

Perry   Believe.

Emile   I thought he was skankin us.

Clinton   Sounded like yu knew, a minute ago.

Perry   Bwoi sweatin now.

Clinton   Must be.

Emile   About wat?

Perry   I know my man Dwayne longer than yu, Emile.

Emile   Yer point is?

Clinton   Leave him, cous, his time comin.

Perry   Yu know.

Emile   Speak English, yu fools.

Perry   Dwayne comin fer yu now, rude bwoi, when yu least expect it. Him comin fer yu. Yu challenged him.

Exit **Perry** *and* **Clinton**.

Ronnie   Oh man, yu fucked up!

Shanice   Shut up, Ronnie.

Ronnie   Tell me now, if dat aint wat he did.

Emile   I don't business.

Shanice   Emile.

Emile   Let him come, I had him before.

Shanice   Listen to me.

Emile   I'll tek him again, let him come.

Ronnie   Yu sweatin big time, Emile.

Shanice   Clean up.

Ronnie   Yu know he's got a gun now.

Emile   Move.

Ronnie   I've seen it. Watch him put a hole in yer head.

Shanice   Enuff.

Emile   Dis is a test.

Shanice   Emile man.

Emile   I'm ready fer him. I aint tekin any more of dis, I aint tekin it from nobody.

Shanice   Yu best listen to me now.

Emile   Yu want me, Dwayne! Well, I'm ready now. Come fer me now!

Shanice   Yu gotta go.

Emile   Don't start.

Shanice   No. Leave.

Emile   Wat do I have to go fer? It's Dwayne dass gotta go. He's goin. And if Perry and Clinton don't like it, they can go too. He's the one who's soff, I tell him who's soff. Me. Emile. Say summin. I defended yu. Tell him yu my woman. No one sexes yu.

Shanice   He only backed off cos yu had a knife, wat happens if Ronnie's right, wat if he's got a gun now?

Ronnie   He has!

Emile   It'll be awright.

Shanice   No, it won't.

Emile   Why yu love to piss on everythin I do?

Shanice   Ca yu don't think.

Emile   I dealt wid him. Like I said.

Shanice   I meant talk.

Emile   Deh yu go again, wid dis talk business.

Shanice   Prove yer better dan him.

Emile   Yu mad or wat?

Shanice   Dan all a dem.

Ronnie   He's gonna kill him.

Shanice   Ronnie!

Ronnie   It's true and yu know it, man. Run and hide, Emile, cos Dwayne is gonna fuck yu up.

Shanice   I'll come wid yu.

Ronnie   Shanice man.

Shanice   Quiet! (*To* **Emile**.) We'll go anyware. We'll leave now, yeah. Right now, come. Emile?

Emile   Dis was supposed to be my time. It was me who had Kwame, not dem. Deh jealous.

Ronnie   Fool.

Shanice   Yu don't have time fer dis.

Emile   They love to put me down, love to mek joke. Do they wake up every night, seein his face?

Ronnie   I thought yu said the nightmares were gone. Aint so big now.

Shanice   Do yu wanna die, Ronnie?

Ronnie   Oh bloody hell, Shanice.

Shanice   Do yu wanna die? Shut yer hole! Emile, ware yu goin?

Emile   It's my time.

Shanice   No.

Emile   I don't business!

Exit **Emile**.

Ronnie   Yu were gonna go?

Shanice   Ronnie man!

Ronnie   Without me?

Shanice   We aint even blood, wass up wid yu?

Ronnie   Yu go, they'll know it was him.

Shanice   And if we stay, he's dead.

Ronnie   Juss don't leave without me, yeah? Shanice?

Shanice   Beg yu, girl, get a life.

Ronnie   I hate it when yu come like dis. Look yer nose down.

Shanice   Calm down.

Ronnie   Plannin on goin without tellin me.

Shanice   I was gonna tell yer.

Ronnie   Yu lie bad. Yu love to lie.

Shanice   Fine, if dass wat yu tink.

Ronnie   And yer still a ho.

Shanice   I dunno wat I am.

Ronnie   Yer a ho, Shanice. Love to have man fuss over yu. Yu get all moist cos of it.

Shanice   Ronnie?

Ronnie   Don't Ronnie me. Go run off wid dat fool, run! I tek care of myself, I don't need yu.

Shanice   Are yu done? Come here.

Ronnie   Fer wat?

Shanice   Come here.

Ronnie   Yu go slap me?

Shanice   I'll slap yu if yu don't come here.

Ronnie *approaches.* **Shanice** *kisses her on the forehead.*

Shanice Don't ever chat fuck ries in my . . . .

Ronnie . . . In my face again, yeah, watever.

Shanice I'd never set out to hurt yu.

Ronnie Yu aint goin.

Shanice I have to.

Ronnie Not without me.

Shanice Deh's gonna come a day, when yu have to look after yerself, Ronnie.

Ronnie I don't care.

Shanice I don't have time fer dis.

Ronnie I'll do it.

Shanice Wat?

Ronnie I'll tell dem wat I saw. I'll get the money, den we can both go.

Shanice Ronnie!

Ronnie If Emile's in prison, Dwayne can't hurt him. Right? Am I right? Well, deh yu go den, problem solved. I'll tell the police, Dwayne can't hurt Emile, den we can go. Yer up fer it? Shanice? Are yu up fer it?

Shanice He wanted to be a designer.

Ronnie Stop goin on about him. He was a smartarse.

Shanice So he had it comin, he deserved to get beat up?

Ronnie Don't yell at me.

Shanice It's not right. Wat 'appened to him weren't right, he didn't deserve to have us comin into his life, man, endin it fer him. It's not right, and no one's sayin it.

Ronnie I'm sayin it.

Shanice Yu want the money.

Ronnie   Was it yu who saw him gettin kicked in the head? Lyin on the ground bleedin, cryin fer his mum? I don't think so. Let me tell the police. Yu want Emile alive and in prison, or dead? It's a good plan, Shanice, it'll work. Please! Let me. Yeah? Yeah?

Shanice   Awright.

Ronnie   Awright wat?

Shanice   Yes, go on, do it.

Exit **Shanice** *and* **Ronnie**.

Enter **Dwayne**, **Perry** *and* **Clinton**.

Perry   Yu shoulda had his claart deh and den.

Clinton   Juss tell me ware and when yer gonna do it, Dwayne. Please. Ca I wanna see dat fool on his hands and knees, cryin like a gal in front of my laughin face, before yu kill him. Please, Dwayne, tell me, a favour to me, man.

Perry   He heard yu, Clinton.

Clinton   Well, tell him to speak up den, can't hear him.

Perry   Dwayne?

Dwayne   Yeah, man, watever.

Clinton   Thank yu. I dunno why yu let it get dis far.

Dwayne   Yu my mum?

Clinton   He pulled a knife on yu, dread, shoulda taken care of business deh and den.

Dwayne   He proved his worth, I thought he was due.

Clinton   Now he's tekin the piss.

Dwayne   Who yu barkin at?

Clinton   Awright, man, ease up.

Dwayne   Yu wanna come it as well, Clinton?

Clinton   All I said was . . .

Dwayne   Don't say anytin.

Perry   Clinton, leave us alone fer a minute, yeah.

Clinton   I didn't say nuttin . . .

Perry   Juss go stand over deh. (*To* **Dwayne**.) So, wat?

Dwayne   Guy gives me a headache wid his voice, man.

Perry   Try livin wid it. Yu go tek care of Emile, everytin sweet, yeah?

Dwayne   Yeah.

Perry   Cool. Crack a smile fer me nuh, man. I tell yu wat though. When dat fool's gone, Shanice.

Perry   It's me and her, man. Trust.

Dwayne   No.

Perry   Wat yu mean, no?

Dwayne   I mean, no. She's off limits, before and after, yu understand?

Perry   Don't tell me yer still sweet fer her? It is, ennit?

Dwayne   None of yer business.

Clinton   Oh man.

Perry   Wat yu want?

Clinton   Yer dad, Dwayne.

Dwayne   Oh man.

Enter **Manny**.

Manny   Good evenin, gentlemen. Wat say yu?

Clinton   Bwoi! (*Waves the air.*)

Perry   Bredren!

Manny   Yu don't have a hug fer yer Uncle Manny?

Perry   I'm awright, Manny, juss stand over deh please.

Manny   Who loves yu more than me?

Clinton   Don't touch me, yeah.

Manny   Bwoi, yu can't say hello?

Dwayne   Hello.

Manny   My bwoi, yu nuh, my bwoi.

Dwayne   Yeah, they know.

Manny   Yu have a pound fer me? Juss a pound, bwoi, please.

Dwayne   Wat yu want it fer?

Manny   I have to go see my mudda, yer granmudda, I need bus fare.

Dwayne   Yeah.

Manny   Gimme a pound please.

Perry   Dwayne, we're not here now, catch yu later, yeah. Let's go up west, catch a bus.

Clinton   Yu get it, I'll walk.

Perry   Yu want walk all the way up west?

Clinton   I don't mind, it keep me fit. Seriously.

Manny   Son?

Perry   Why can't yu jus say it?

Clinton   Say wat?

Perry   We have to go through dis every time.

Clinton   Say wat?

Perry   Yer skint.

Clinton   I aint skint.

Manny   Listen.

Perry   Yu want me to pay fer yer bus fare.

Clinton   If yu want to pay fer me, dass up to yu, ennit.

Perry   Clinton! Juss say it.

Clinton   Awright. I'll come wid yu, if yu don't want to come on the bus by yerself.

Perry   Shut up will yu please, can yu do dat? Shut up. Hold up. Yu got money, from the purse.

Clinton   Yeah I got money, but I aint got change fer the bus.

Perry   Yu woulda walked all the way up west, even though yu have money?

Clinton   I don't have change.

Perry   Yu are gone, Clinton man, yu are so far gone.

Exit **Perry** *and* **Clinton**.

Manny   Hey, yu my bwoi, yu nuh.

Dwayne   Don't touch me.

Manny   Juss gimme two pound.

Dwayne   Yu said one pound.

Manny   Two pound fer me, please.

Dwayne   Do yu even know wat yer sayin, half the time?

Manny   Yu my bwoi.

Dwayne   Go brush yer teet, man.

Manny   Juss gimme sum change. Yes, yes. Hey, let me have sum more of dem silver ones yeah, please.

Dwayne   Take it all. Juss take it.

Manny   My bwoi.

Dwayne   Two words fer yu yeah, please. Soap and water.

Manny   Yu my bwoi.

Dwayne   Yeah, yeah.

Manny   Yu my bwoi. Good bwoi, Junior.

Dwayne   Wat?

Manny   Wat?

Dwayne   Wat did yu juss call me?

Manny   Yu my bwoi.

Dwayne   Yu juss called me Junior.

Manny   Nuh, man.

Dwayne   I aint deaf, yu called me Junior.

Manny   Junior? Who dat?

Dwayne   Who is Junior? Did I hear yu right? Who is Junior?

Manny   Bwoi?

Dwayne   Junior is yer son, who live up by Shepherd's Bush, my half-brudda, dass who Junior is. Junior live wid his two little sistas, Tasha and Caroline, yer daughters, my half-sistas! Remember dem? Nuh, it muss be Anton yu remember, yer son who live up by Dagenham way. Or is it Stuart, my little brudda, who live two minutes away from my yard, who I never see. Nuh, nuh, it muss be the latest one, dat lickle baby wid the stupid name, Kenisha. Wass my name?

Manny   Bwoi?

Dwayne   Move yer hand away from me. Wass my name? Yer so drunk, yu don't even know which yout of yours yer chattin to. Wass my name? Say my name before I buss yer claart all over dis street. Say it.

Manny   Dwayne. It's Dwayne, yer name Dwayne.

Dwayne   Yu musta bin beggin to God, to tell yu.

Manny   Yu Dwayne.

Dwayne   Get off me.

Manny   The one in trouble.

Dwayne   Who tell yu I was in trouble?

Manny   It was yu who beat up dat bwoi, weren't it?
Weren't it?

Dwayne   It weren't me dat beat him right.

Manny   One a yer friends den.

Dwayne   Who tell yu?

Manny   Everyone know, 'bout who tell me? See, I do
know yu. I know my own children right, I know! Don't tell
me I don't know.

Dwayne   So, wat yu gonna do?

Manny   Why yu do it, son?

Dwayne   Answer my question first. I didn't do it, I told
yu. So, wat yu gonna do? Wat yu gonna do?

Manny   Yu shame me.

Dwayne   Yu want chat 'bout shame? Shame is seein yu,
in the off-licence tryin to buy a can of beer wid only twenty
pence in yer hand. Beggin dat Indian man to let yu have it.

Manny   So wat, yu gonna mess up yer life?

Dwayne   Wat are yu gonna do?

Manny   Yu mad?

Dwayne   Wat are yu gonna do?

Manny   Dwayne?

Dwayne   Wat are yu gonna do? Wat are yu gonna do?
Wat are yu gonna do?

Exit **Dwayne** *and* **Manny**.

Enter **Joe**, **Matt** *and* **Ronnie**.

Ronnie   Is dat it?

Joe   Not quite.

Ronnie   So, when I get my money?

Joe   Hey.

Ronnie   Wat?

Matt   Why do they call you troll? Can't be nice.

Ronnie   Wat yu think?

Matt   Do they call you it? The boys?

Ronnie   Not just dem.

Matt   Is that why you're here?

Ronnie   Wat?

Matt   To get back at them.

Ronnie   No.

Matt   Get them into trouble.

Ronnie   No.

Matt   You had better tell us the truth now.

Ronnie (*to* **Joe**)   Him deaf?

Joe   Answer his question.

Ronnie   I just did.

Matt   This is a serious allegation you're making.

Ronnie   I know.

Matt   I want you to be sure now.

Ronnie   I am, I saw dem kill him. I thought they were
jackin him at first. They were standin around him, in a
circle, scarin him. They were shoutin and laughin, darin
Emile to beat him, so he did.

Matt   Did what?

Ronnie   Kicked him. He was kickin him in the head.

Matt   Anything else?

Ronnie   One a dem, I think it was Perry, knocked off his glasses.

Matt   What else?

Ronnie   I saw dem run off. I ran too, in the opposite direction.

Matt   What else?

Ronnie   What else wat? I saw him beat him, Emile beat him up, they run off. Wat? Wat!

Joe   Tell me about the trainers.

Ronnie   Whose trainers? My trainers?

Joe   Kwame's trainers.

Ronnie   His?

Joe   Yes!

Ronnie   Oh, right!

Joe   Well?

Matt   Ronnie?

Ronnie   Wat?

Matt   We're waiting.

Ronnie   Cool. (*Nervous laughter.*)

Joe   Listen to me, Ronnie, yeah. You told us all about what you saw, Kwame gettin attacked, that's good, that's all good. But we still need you to help us clear up a few things. Such as the trainers, Kwame's trainers. You saw them take them off him, right, right?

Matt   Joe?

90　Fallout

Ronnie　Right, yeah, I saw dat. They took the trainers off him.

Joe　Before or after he was attacked, Ronnie?

Ronnie　Before. It was before.

Joe　Good. That was all I wanted to know. When I turn on the tape, yeah . . .

Matt　I need to speak with you.

Joe　. . . That's what yer going to tell me. Right?

Ronnie　Cool.

Matt　Joe!

Exit **Ronnie**.

Tell me you didn't just do that.　*[handwritten: Question animatedly]*

Joe　Believe.

Matt　She had no idea what you were talking about.　*[handwritten: Inform simply]*

Joe　That's not how I read it.

Matt　We held back that info about the trainers, for a reason.　*[handwritten: Inform exasperatedly]*

Joe　Yeah yeah yeah.

Matt　She didn't see a thing.　*[handwritten: Inform reefully]*

Joe　She must have done.

Matt　Her story was all over the place.　*[handwritten: Inform angrily]*

Joe　So she couldn't strings two sentences together, so what? It's the way those kids talk. You're treating them like they don't belong. That's how they feel, they're not stupid.

Matt　Do you have any idea what will happen if we screw this? Do you? Disciplinary, desk jobs. Promotions, chances fucked.　*[handwritten: Question rhetorical]*

Joe　She knew about the BMW.

[handwritten left margin: Shouldn't have told her.]
[handwritten left margin: consequences / screwed]

Matt That was in the local paper.

Joe She saw it happen. We got him, what did I say. You don't like it, you should have spoken up, Sarge!

Matt So it's Sarge now, is it? You had no right leading a witness like that, without consulting me.

Joe I didn't think you'd be comfortable with it.

Matt Do not patronise me!

Joe You telling me you haven't bent a few rules in yer time?

Matt Of course I have. What kind of a wanker have you got me down as?

Joe So you'd fit up some white kid? Oh, but this is different though, ennit?

Matt You know it is.

Joe A black kid. You have to watch yourself. Got be Mr Politically Correct Man of the Year.

Matt You juss won't give that up. You have done nothing but push me and push me.

Joe So push me back.

Matt I have had enough.

Joe It should only matter if it's true.

Matt I won't have it.

Joe You know he did it.

Matt Course I know.

Joe So, what?

Matt So I need to think, is that alright with you?

Joe There are two kinds of people.

Matt Are you going to let me think?

Joe   Ones that break the law, ones that don't. I'm just dealing with the ones that do.

Matt   What do you think I'm trying to do?

Joe   Prove it.

Matt   Why do you hate them so much?

Joe   Prove it.

Matt   It's really got to hurt that you're not black enough for them.

Joe   Wass this fool going on with?

Matt   Joe, I'm warning you.

Joe   I'm gone.

Matt   Answer my question.

Joe   You think you can get to me like this?

Matt   I'm not trying to get to you, I want you to answer my question. They're your people, why do you hate them?

Joe   Listen, yeah, those boys are not my people. You think I care what they think?

Matt   Yes, I do think you care. 'Big time policeman, look at me now.'

Joe   (*laughs*)   Go, Matt.

Matt   You were Kwame. Weren't you? Look, I'm sorry, Joe.

Joe   Hey, don't you dare apologise to me. Don't turn soff now. Just keep your *Guardian*-reading shit to one side, yeah, or whatever it is you read . . .

Matt   I'm not like that!

Joe   You fucking people!

Matt   That is enough, Constable!

Joe   Wid your wishy-washy liberal crap. Are you so afraid to say what you really feel?

Matt   I know what you want me to say.

Joe   So say it.

Matt   No.

Joe   Give me back the old school of police. Give them boys something to really cry about.

Matt   Not another word.

Joe   At least they'd know where they stand.

Matt   Don't push me.

Joe   To do what? To say what?

Matt   Leave it.

Joe   Come on, Matt, let them know where they stand. That's all they want.

Matt   Is that what you want, Joe?

Joe   This isn't about me.

Matt   You don't know where you stand?

Joe   All yer doin is cloudin the issue.

Matt   And you're running away. You're hiding. Alright, you want to hear about the time when I was in uniform, when I had to stop my first black person?

Joe   Yes.

Matt   He had a defective headlamp, I waved him down in the middle of the night, he comes out of his car screaming, I'm only picking on him cos he's black. He was doing forty. How the hell did I know what colour he was? All I saw was a defective headlamp.

Joe   Dumb nigger. Worst kind.

Matt   But that's not what I thought. He was a prat. A stupid ignorant prat. That's what I thought, it's what I said. I got a reprimand.

Joe *claps slowly.*

[handwritten margin note: I won't say it.]

Matt   There's no clouding of the issue for me, Joe. You'll never get me to say it. I don't want to say it. I'm not going to feel bad for what I believe in, and I do believe in it. The job, wishy-washy views, everything.

Joe   He's going to walk then.

Matt   You don't know that, that's not up to you.

Joe   Are you going to man up or what?

[handwritten margin note: DIs (all)]

Matt   It's not our call. We'll let the DI decide if we have enough to charge him with, alright? And you're lucky, I'm not going to mention what you just did.

Joe   Well, thanks.

Matt   You can fuck off, I'm not doing it for you. Because, you see, Joe, I know where I stand. Now I'm going to tell you where you stand. Right here, beside me with your mouth shut.

Joe *goes to leave.*

[handwritten margin note: Dominant Matt]

Matt   You move one more inch, and you're finished. You speak when I say, you do as I say. Is that clear enough for you, Constable? This is what you wanted, to be like everyone else. Well, come on then, crack a smile, Joe. That's an order.

Exit **Joe** *and* **Matt**.

Enter **Dwayne** *and* **Shanice**.

Shanice   So it's true?

Dwayne   Wat?

Shanice   Yu have a gun.

Dwayne   Maybe. Wat yu want?

Shanice   Yu know wat I want.

Dwayne   Beggin aint yer style, Shanice.

Shanice   Juss leave him.

Dwayne   He call me a liar.

Shanice   So wat?

Dwayne   I'm takin dat, yu mad? Yu best find a new boyfriend.

Shanice   Big man.

Dwayne   Like yu know me.

Shanice   I know yu. Cryin yer eyes out all the way home from school, when yer were twelve, cos yu wet yerself, dass who I know.

Dwayne   Wat yu see in him?

Shanice   We both want summin else.

Dwayne   And I don't?

Shanice   Yu?

Dwayne   Yu see!

Shanice   Bwoi, yu tryin to tell me summin? Wat? Why am I standin here?

Dwayne   Bye.

Shanice   Yu aint gonna do nuttin.

Dwayne   Is who yu darin me?

Shanice   Yer soff.

Dwayne   Is who are yu?

Shanice   Can't yu see wat he's doin?

Dwayne   Playin big man.

Shanice   Like yu.

Dwayne   I'm better.

Shanice   Let me have him.

Dwayne   Ware yu gonna go?

Shanice   Sumware.

Dwayne   Yu aint gonna go. Yu aint.

Shanice   Gonna miss me, Dwayne?

Dwayne   See yu. Love to flirt.

Shanice   Yu can't say it.

Dwayne   I aint backin down, Shanice, he dissed me.

Shanice   Yes yu can.

Dwayne   Don't chat rubbish to me. Why him? Wat is special 'bout him?

Shanice   He's the first one to ask me out.

Dwayne   I've asked yu out.

Shanice   He didn't juss yank my arm, and say, come!

Dwayne   I bet he can't even kiss.

Shanice   Him kiss better than yu. When we first went out, I knew he wanted to put his arm round me, I look at him, and goes, get on wid it. He was so shy.

Dwayne   Soff.

Shanice   He asked if he could kiss me.

Dwayne   Him a bwoi!

Shanice   He asked me, Dwayne.

Dwayne   Yu don't ask to kiss, yu juss kiss.

Shanice   I couldn't believe it.

Dwayne   Ca yer a slapper.

Shanice   Dass why I went wid yu. Ca I didn't want to believe it. Whenever anyone says I'm good, or nice, I don't wanna believe it.

Dwayne   I wanna kiss yu.

Shanice   Wat?

Dwayne   Is that awright?

Shanice   Yu mad?

Dwayne *kisses her.*

Shanice   Wanna grind me as well now, Dwayne?

Dwayne   No. (*Strokes her face.*)

Enter **Emile**.

Emile   So now wat, yu want me to beat him up now?

Dwayne   Come.

Shanice   Emile, no.

Emile   Why?

Shanice   Cos he'll kill yu.

Dwayne   No, let him come.

Emile   He was sexin yu, like Kwame, I have to.

Dwayne   So, come. (*Pulls out gun.*) My friend here waitin fer yu, come.

Shanice   Dwayne, back off, man, please.

Dwayne   Tell yer bwoi first.

Shanice   Put the gun down, wass wrong wid yu?

Emile   I can get a gun too, Dwayne.

Dwayne   Is it?

Emile   Believe.

Shanice   STOP! Dwayne man?

Dwayne Yu love to think I won't do it.

Shanice I know yu can do it, I know yu will do it. But I'm askin yu, I'm beggin yu, yeah, please don't do it. (*Beat.*) Emile, come on, man, yu don't want to do dis.

Emile Well, stop makin me. It's yu dass makin me, it's yu dass makin me do dis.

Dwayne Yer soff.

Emile I might as well fling yu at him.

Dwayne Yer givin me yer gal, Emile, cheers.

Emile Yu love to have man chase yu.

Shanice Awright, do it, fight him, go fight him, kill each oder ca I don't business no more, bloody fight him.

Dwayne Come.

Shanice He's waitin.

Dwayne Yu comin or wat, Emile? I tell yu wat, I let yu mek a move first, yeah?

Shanice Emile?

Dwayne Come!

Shanice He aint.

Dwayne Ca him soff.

Shanice Dwayne, juss leave us, yeah.

Dwayne Yu best start runnin.

Exit **Dwayne**.

Emile Well, go on den.

Shanice Wat?

Emile Go follow him.

Shanice Go follow him ware, Emile? I told yu not to hang round wid him. I told yu wat he was like.

Emile   First Kwame, now him.

Shanice   No. Kwame weren't tryin to sex me.

Emile   Shut up.

Shanice   He was juss bin nice. He didn't do anythin, he weren't after anythin.

Emile   Yu told me.

Shanice   I know wat I told yu.

Emile   So, why?

Shanice   Yu made me feel special, I weren't juss sum yattie to yu. Dwayne comes along, and yu stop noticin me. Yu were too busy impressin him. Yu made me lose faith, not juss in yu, but in me, man. So I goes, fuck yu, Emile, fuck yu. I thought Kwame fancied me, so I thought yes! I'll rush dat.

Emile   He did try and sex yu.

Shanice   Hello!! I tried to sex him, he blew me off, Emile. Ca he was nice! Juss nice.

Emile   Yu?

Shanice   Ronnie's gone to the police. I told her to. Don't look at me like dat. Yu were supposed to juss give him a slap or summin. Why yu have to kill him?

Emile *grabs her.*

Shanice   It's dis place! Let's go, right now, come. I'll look after yu. Ronnie, she's so stupid, man, she thinks we're gonna run off togeder wid the reward money. Yer the one I want to run off wid. Yu were right all the time. I can't keep lookin after her, I don't want to. Yu aint got a choice no more. Emile!

Exit **Shanice** *and* **Emile**.

Enter **Ronnie**, **Matt** *and* **Joe**.

Ronnie   And I want a room wid cable.

Matt   Don't start.

Ronnie   It best have a tele wid cable.

Matt   You might have a video.

Ronnie   I want DVD.

Matt   What's the difference?

Ronnie   Obvious yu don't have one.

Matt   You will go where we put you.

Ronnie   Yu joke.

Matt   So be quiet.

Ronnie (*to* **Joe**)   Yu gonna let dis geezer chat to me like dat?

Matt   Take it or leave it.

Ronnie   I'll leave it den.

Matt   Where do you think you're going?

Ronnie   Home.

Matt   That is the last place you want to be, Veronica.

Ronnie   It's Ronnie, how hard is it to say dat, Ronnie!

Matt   Alright, Ronnie. I don't think you realise how serious this is.

Ronnie   I do.

Matt   You are, potentially, an important witness in a murder investigation.

Ronnie   Yeah, yeah. Love to go on.

Matt   What do you think your friends would do if you went home?

Ronnie I don't know, go mad fer me, ennit? (*Laughs.*) Call me troll, I don't care. Used to it. Don't care wat they think. Except Shanice, but she knows why I'm doing it, she knows.

Matt This is as serious as it gets. Right, Constable?

Joe *nods his head.*

Matt Right, Ronnie?

Ronnie Yes! Awright. Bloody hell.

Matt So we'll have no more talk about cable TV, MTV base, DV bloody Ds, PlayStation.

Ronnie PlayStation 2, actually. Get it right. Joke!

Matt Constable?

Joe Hold it down, yeah.

Ronnie Why don't yu kiss his arse while yer at it.

Joe Just ease up, OK.

Ronnie Yu white man's bitch.

Joe This is it for you.

Ronnie So I'm supposed to stay in sum room and do nish?

Matt We can take you out.

Ronnie When do I get my money?

Matt You know when.

Ronnie You can't even dash me a few dollars till den?

Matt That is not up to me.

Ronnie Can I use a phone?

Matt Who do you want to call?

Ronnie Shanice.

Joe Why Shanice?

Ronnie   Tell her I'm awright.

Matt   I think your mind should be on other things.

Ronnie   I want call Shanice. I want a McDonald's Happy Meal.

Matt   Later.

Ronnie   I'm hungry, dread.

Matt   I said later. We're expecting company. Our Inspector would like to speak with you.

Ronnie   Why yu lot love to ask borin questions?

Matt   Hey!

Ronnie   Awright.

Joe   Ronnie?

Ronnie   Wat?

Joe   Come on, just behave yourself, please.

Ronnie   I said awright.

Joe   This is important.

Ronnie   I know.

Joe   Right!

Ronnie   Yes, man!

Matt   This is hopeless.

Ronnie   Yu want calm down, dread. Can I have my McDonald's now?

Enter the **Inspector**.

Inspector   How far away were you?

Ronnie   A bit.

Inspector   A bit what? Give it to me in yards.

Ronnie   I dunno, juss a bit. I can't remember exactly.

Inspector   Well, you will have to remember.

Ronnie   Wat fer? I don't know.

Inspector   How could you forget that?

Ronnie   I didn't forget, I said I don't know.

Inspector   The point I am trying to make, Veronica . . .

Ronnie   Ronnie.

Inspector   . . . If you were there . . .

Ronnie   I was.

Inspector   . . . I do not think it is something you could forget.

Ronnie   Love to chat.

Inspector   Listen to me, you may find this amusing, Veronica . . .

Ronnie   Ronnie! Yu deaf?

Inspector   . . . I can assure you, those people in the courtroom will not.

Ronnie   Watever.

Inspector   You thought there was a robbery going on over the street, that they were 'jackin' somebody?

Ronnie   Yeah.

Inspector   You were standing behind the bus-stop shelter, across the road?

Ronnie   Yeah. Bloody hell.

Inspector   And you were hiding behind the bus-stop shelter because you did not want the boys to see you.

Ronnie   Dwayne don't like it when I'm followin him.

Inspector   Yes or no?

Ronnie   Yeah.

Inspector   Now, at that point in the evening . . .

Ronnie   Yer talkin too fast again.

Inspector   . . . At, that, point, in the evening, a silver BMW pulls up, by the bus stop, the window of the front-passenger side rolls down, a young white woman leans out, and you have a conversation with this woman.

Ronnie   Yeah.

Inspector   She asked if you lived in the area.

Ronnie   Yeah.

Inspector   She asked you for directions.

Ronnie   Yeah, yeah, yeah!

Inspector   Whilst Emile and his friends were attacking Kwame?

Ronnie   Yes. (*Aside.*) Slag.

Inspector   I beg your pardon?

Joe   Ronnie!

Ronnie   Nuttin.

Inspector   Furthermore, the music playing from the car radio is rather loud.

Ronnie   At first, but her man turned it down.

Inspector   But you could still hear the music?

Ronnie   Yeah, it was Jay Z.

Inspector   I'm sorry?

Ronnie   Jay Z the rapper. Dass who was playin on the radio. Are we done now?

Inspector   Not yet. Now help me out here. Despite the conversation, despite the 'Jay Z' music playing from the car radio, you were not distracted at all, from witnessing the attack?

Ronnie   No.

Inspector   And the boys do not notice that you are watching them?

Ronnie   No.

Inspector   You didn't hear about the BMW from the newspaper, did you?

Ronnie   No.

Inspector   But you knew we were looking for it, so did you decide to use it, to make your story more credible?

Ronnie   No.

Inspector   Did you really speak to that woman?

Ronnie   Why she carryin on?

Inspector   Did you see those boys?

Ronnie   Callin me a liar.

Inspector   I need you to be absolutely sure about this.

Ronnie   I thought yu wanted me to help?

Inspector   So you weren't following the events in the newspaper quite closely then?

Ronnie   No.

Inspector   You weren't desperate to grab the opportunity, to be the centre of attention?

Ronnie   Look, I might have glanced at summin in the paper, yeah.

Inspector   So, you do admit to lying?

Ronnie   Everyone was readin it. It had a picture of our estate and dat, it was cool.

Inspector   You didn't do more than read?

Ronnie   Why, why would I, wass so special about him?

Inspector   Twenty thousand pounds?

Ronnie   Oh man, I've had enough of dis. I'm done.

Joe   Come on, Ronnie!

Inspector (*to* **Matt**)   Yes, thank you, Constable. Sit down, Veronica.

Ronnie   Call me dat one more time.

Inspector   Sit down please. Just tell us the truth.

Ronnie   I am tellin yu the truth.

Inspector   I don't think you are.

Ronnie   I don't care.

Inspector   You were lying when you said you were on the street.

Ronnie   No.

Inspector   You were lying about seeing what happened, you know everyone is going to be watching you.

Ronnie   Yer point?

Inspector   You love it.

Ronnie   No I don't.

Inspector   You will love anything that will stop you from being reminded of what you really are, a sad, lonely little girl, with no friends.

Ronnie   I've got loads of friends. Shanice is my friend.

Inspector   What is your nickname? What do your friends call you?

Ronnie   I'm tellin the bloody truth, is dis wat happens when yu tell the truth? Well, fuck dat!

Inspector Calm down please.

Ronnie Try and help the police, say wat they want me to say, dis is the thanks I get.

Inspector What was that? What was it that we told you to say? Ronnie?

Joe Awright, look, I made a mistake, yeah.

Inspector Quiet.

Joe It's my fault.

Inspector Sergeant?

Joe But she saw him kill him.

Matt Joe?

Joe She saw the boy do it.

Matt Don't.

Ronnie Him goin mad or wat?

Joe Tell her, Ronnie, tell her what it felt like seeing Kwame lying there on the ground, how it made you feel. That it made you care. Tell her.

Ronnie Is who yu screamin at?

Inspector Look at me, Ronnie. I said look at me.

Ronnie This is fuck ries.

Inspector What did they tell you to say?

Ronnie Dat I saw dem tek the trainers.

Inspector You said before you saw them do that.

Ronnie I know. Musta happened when I was talkin to dat woman, ennit?

Inspector So, you were distracted.

Ronnie No. Fer a second, yeah.

Joe   Shit.

Inspector   You have just lied to me. If we had put you in a courtroom, you would have committed perjury.

Ronnie   I'm not lyin. I saw dem do it, man. I saw dem kill him. Yu know wat they'll do to me if I go back home? How can I be lyin?

Inspector   I see.

Ronnie   Yu don't bloody see. Yu don't see us. None of yer. 'Bout yu see! I aint lyin.

Inspector (*to* **Joe** *and* **Matt**)   You cannot be serious.

Joe   Ma'am?

Inspector   Not another word. You've got nothing.

Ronnie   So we done now? Are we done?

Inspector   Get her out of here.

Ronnie (*pleads*)   Shanice!

Exit **Inspector**, **Ronnie** *and* **Matt**.

Enter **Emile**.

Joe   See, Emile, dis is gettin vex! I wanna tell you something, yeah? Cos, that's all I got time for now, thanks to that little friend of yours, that troll. One time, when I was in uniform, yeah, early in the afternoon, it was 'bout four or summin, got a call, two pissheads fighting outside a pub, one black, one white. One a dem spilled the other one's drink, I couldn't remember who, whatever. Anyhow, they were having a right go at each other. Pushing, and sum shoving. Both a them are as bad as each other, effing and blinding, tellin you! I didn't want to get involved. Shitting myself, if truth be told. But I stepped in, arrested them both, boom boom! (*Slaps* **Emile**.) The white guy, calmed himself down, straight off, he stood there, knew he was in the wrong, didn't even try to run off. Black guy, different story. He couldn't stop mouthing off to me. What do you think he said, guess.

Emile   Dunno.

Joe   Cocksucker. Pig. Bastard. Traitor to my own, white man's bitch. The lot. Goin on about, how I was only nickin him cos he was black and I want to be white. By the time we got him back to the station, he was still carrying on. Still shoutin, mekin up all kinds of noise. It took five of us to throw him in a cell. (*Slaps* **Emile**.) You know what the white guy was doing during all this? Nothing, nish. From the time I showed up on the street, to when we got back to the station, he didn't say a word. And he was the one throwing out the most licks, when they were havin the fight. You see wat I mean, Emile? (*Slaps him.*) You see where I'm goin wid this? White man get caution, get sent home the very same day, black man spend the rest of the day and night in the cell, cos he couldn't keep his stupid wurtless mout shut, couldn't play the game! White man played the game, played it beautifully, I wanted to shake his hand and go, 'Yeah, nuff respect.' I tell you, Emile, when it comes to that, them white bwois are poles apart. Niggers, Emile, can't play the game. You can't play the game, Kwame played the game, Kwame had a life. He was a decent kid. But you, you! (*Slaps him repeatedly.*) You want a life, bwoi, get yer own. Why you have to tek his? You know what, it's fuckers like you, like that pisshead, is why I had to leave. Now it's fuckers like you that bring me back to where I started. You had to drag me down, ennit? You had to drag Kwame down. You feel good about that? You love that? Is it? Do you? Do you? (*Slaps him.*) Do you?

Enter **Shanice**.

Joe   Yer wurtless!!

Shanice (*stands between* **Joe** *and* **Emile**)   Leave him.

Joe   Shanice, move.

Shanice   Are yu mad?

Joe   Move.

Shanice   Leave him.

Joe   I'm letting him know where he stands.

Shanice   Yu think dis is gonna change him?

Joe   Bwoi drowning, girl.

Shanice   Wat else yu expect him to be?

Joe   You want drown too?

Shanice   Wat yu know about him? Wat yu know about me?

Emile   Get off.

Shanice   Emile?

Emile   Leave me!

Exit **Emile**.

Joe   Where you goin?

Shanice   Nigger, yu best step back.

Joe   Don't go after him, Shanice, remember your gran. He aint even sorry for wat he did.

Shanice   Yu don't know him.

Joe   I know him.

Shanice   Yu don't know him.

Joe   Fine, go drown with the idiot.

Shanice   Wat about yu, yu sorry? Yu sorry fer wat yu did, Joe? Say yer sorry, say it.

Joe   Sorry for what? You know what him and that friend of yours have done to me? You want drown yerself, go.

Shanice   Yu go. Carryin on like we should tek after yu, why should we be like yu?

Exit **Joe**.

(*Aside.*) Yer fool.

Enter **Manny**.

Manny   Hey, pretty gal.

Shanice   Oh please.

Manny   Yu know yu love me.

Shanice   Is it?

Manny   Yu have a pound fer me? Beg yu fer a pound, please.

Shanice   Do yu even know how to wash yerself?

Manny   Beg yu.

Shanice   Yu stink.

Manny   Juss a pound.

Shanice   Step.

Enter **Dwayne**, *carrying a football.*

Manny   My bwoi, yu awright? Yu have a pound fer me? Beg yu fer a pound. Son? Bwoi?

Exit **Manny**.

Shanice   Yu see how yeller his teet is?

Dwayne   Yu hear from Emile?

Shanice   No.

Dwayne   Yu don't know ware he's gone?

Shanice   Stay wid his sista.

Dwayne   Wat about troll?

Shanice   Gone sumware wid her mum.

Dwayne   I dunno wat she's gonna do without yu.

Shanice   She's gonna have to learn, ennit? They both are. I told her to do it.

Dwayne   I aint here fer dat. Yu don't have to be scared, yeah.

Shanice   I aint.

Dwayne   Yu are. Don't.

Shanice   Fine, I won't.

Dwayne   Did I tell ya? Clinton pass his BTEC.

Shanice *laughs.*

Dwayne (*feeling self-conscious*)   Wat?

Shanice   Nuttin. Dass good. Wat yu doin wid dat?

Dwayne   Wanna show yu summin.

Shanice   Wat?

Dwayne (*places football on ground*)   Gonna prove to yu dat third one was no a goal.

Shanice   Oh man, yu are sad.

Dwayne   Scared I'm right, Shanice?

Shanice   No.

Dwayne   So come.

Shanice   It was seven years ago, how am I supposed to remember ware I was, please?

Dwayne   I'm Neil, remember him?

Shanice   Yes.

Dwayne   I'm here.

Shanice   Yeah, and?

Dwayne   Yer outside the box, Perry's in goal, he's clocked yu makin yer move.

Shanice   I knew exactly ware I was gonna shoot.

Dwayne   Bottom right-hand corner.

Shanice   Right.

Dwayne   I'm givin yu chase, tryin to stop yer.

Shanice   But yu can't.

Dwayne   I nearly had yu.

Shanice   Right, den I scored.

Dwayne   No.

Shanice   Rest yer lip 'bout no.

Dwayne   Yu did strike, I'd give yu dat, but it bounced right off Clinton's knee.

Shanice   Deflection. Case rested.

Dwayne   If it hadn't, it woulda gone wide.

Shanice   No.

Dwayne   Tellin yu.

Shanice   Shut up.

Dwayne   Ask Clinton.

Shanice   Dwayne, put the ball down. Put the ball down. Wat are we doin?

Dwayne   Yu really think I woulda shot Emile?

Shanice   Yeah.

Dwayne   Believe.

Shanice   So, wat?

Dwayne   Yu know wat stopped me?

Shanice   Lemme guess, me and my face.

Dwayne   Yeah.

Shanice   Yu fall on yer head or summin?

Dwayne   No.

Shanice   So, wat now?

Dwayne   Go out and dat.

Shanice (*laughs*)   Go out and dat.

Dwayne   Yeah.

Shanice   Awright.

Dwayne   Wat?

Shanice   Yu deaf? I said awright.

Dwayne   Cool.

Shanice   But Dwayne?

Dwayne   Wat?

Shanice   Yu aint grindin me.

Exit

CPSIA information can be obtained
at www.ICGtesting.com
Printed in the USA
LVHW041653191118
597654LV00013B/171/P